C O N T E N T S

Printed and bound by Antony Rowe Ltd, Eastbourne

1153	Pte.	ALBURY George	-	-	Discharge by purchase 30.9.50
1432	Pte.	ALDER John	C	G	Wounded at Chilianwala
634	Pte.	ANDERSON Andrew	C	G	Died 20.11.49
1585	Pte.	BALM George	C	G	Drowned 22.4.49
1601	Pte.	BARRY Henry	C	-	Killed at Chilianwala
1410	Pte.	BECK Thomas	C	G	Discharge by purchase 28.2.50
1793	Pte.	BRETT Nathan	C	-	Killed at Chilianwala
1681	Cpl.	BONSER John	C	G	Discharge free 28.2.51
693	Pte.	BROADWAY John	C	G	Died 4.12.49
1444	Pte.	BROOKES J.	C	G	Died 19.1.51
1706	Pte.	BROOKES Henry	-	-	Inv. 28.8.50 to England 26.2.51
1820	Pte.	BUNN James	C	G	Drowned 14.3.49
1625	Pte.	CHARRINGTON Charles	C	G	Died 27.9.50
1610	Pte.	CHRISTIE George	C	G	Discharge by purchase 30.9.50
581	Pte.	CLARKE Thomas	C	-	Wounded 22.11.48 Died 18.7.51
767	T.S.M.	CLARKE William	C	G	Invalided 20.10.49 Permitted to remain in India
1720	Pte.	COLEMAN Samuel	C	G	Died 5.12.50
1080	Pte.	COLES Henry	C	-	Died 6.9.49
1372	Pte.	COLLIER George B.	C	G	Discharge by purchase 31.3.50
1782	Pte.	COLLIN John	C	G	Wounded at Chilianwala
1790	Pte.	COLLINS James	C	-	Killed at Chilianwala
1521	Pte.	COMBER James	C	-	Killed at Chilianwala
1231	Pte.	COMBES James	C	G	Drowned 14.8.49
1557	Pte.	COX Alfred	C	G	Discharge by purchase 28.2.51
564	Pte.	CRAYDEN Charles	C	G	Discharge by purchase 31.12.49
1528	Pte.	CURTIS John	C	G	Died 31.8.51
1345	Sjt.	CUTTS George	-	-	Discharge by purchase 30.11.50
1871	Cpl.	DAINES William	-	-	Died 24.9.49
1846	Pte.	DOYLE Henry Thomas	C	G	Died 9.11.50
1636	Pte.	DUDLEY DIGGS W.	C	-	Killed at Chilianwala
465	T.S.M.	DYSON Robert	C	G	Died 18.7.49
1598	Pte.	EVANS Joseph	C	G	Discharged
1470	Pte.	EXCELL Henry	C	-	Wounded at Chilianwala
1211	Pte.	FENN Charles	C	G	Wounded at Chilianwala
260	Pte.	FENTON James	C	G	Invalided 24.8.49 to England 7.2.50
1337	Pte.	FIELD S. James	C	-	Discharge by purchase 31.8.49
950	Pte.	FISHER J. Charles	C	G	Died 3.6.49
967	Pte.	FLACK Robert	C	G	Wounded 22.11.48
646	Pte.	FLEMING Robert	C	G	Wounded at Chilianwala, Died 11.10.49
872	Pte.	FRIEND George	C	G	Died 29.6.51
1839	Pte.	GARNER Joseph	-	-	Died 21.12.48
1723	O.R.C.	GRAY William	C	G	Died 22.5.49
1574	Pte.	GRIEVE Ralph	-	-	Died 25.11.48 of wounds rec. in action 22.11.48
1580	Pte.	GRIFFITHS Robert	C	-	Killed at Chilianwala
917	Pte.	HALE Henry	C	-	Killed at Chilianwala
1543	Pte.	HAMILTON John S.	C	-	Killed at Chilianwala
1119	Pte.	HANDY William	C	-	Wounded at Chilianwala

1545	Pte.	HARDING George	C	G	Died 9.9.51
1578	Pte.	HAWBREY William T.	C	-	Wounded at Chilianwala Invalided 16.8.49 To England 7.2.50
975	Pte.	HARRIS Charles	C	G	Died 29.12.50
1334	Pte.	HARRIS Richard	C	G	Discharge by purchase 30.9.50
459	Pte.	HART C. John	C	-	Killed at Chilianwala
1593	Pte.	HART Henry	C	G	Wounded at Chilianwala
1721	Pte.	HICKS George	C	G	Died 28.12.50
885	Pte.	HUBBARD John	C	G	Wounded at Chilianwala
810	Pte.	HUDSON James	C	G	Wounded at Chilianwala
1643	Pte.	HUGHES Michael	-	-	Invalided 16.8.49, to England 7.2.50
1458	Pte.	HUNT James	C	-	Killed at Chilianwala
1579	Pte.	JOHN Thomas	C	-	Died 15.12.49
1888	Pte.	JOHNSON Emanuel	C	-	Killed at Chilianwala
935	Pte.	JONES John (1st)	C	G	Discharge by purchase 31.10.50
1699	Pte.	IRELAND Robert	C	G.	Died 17.5.49
1714	Pte.	KENNEDY William	-	G	Died 29.5.49
825	Pte.	LANGDALE George	C	G	Discharge Free 31.8.49
1860	Pte.	LANGSTON William	C	-	Killed at Chilianwala
1053	Pte.	LINKEN Robert	C	G	Wounded 22.11.48
422	Sjt.	McCASKIE John	C	G	Wounded at Chilianwala, invalided 8.2.49 To England 10.5.49
1570	Pte.	McENERNEY Richard	C	-	Killed at Chilianwala
719	Pte.	McHARG John	C	G	Deserted 11.12.50
427	Pte.	McKINNON Hugh	C	G	Died 4.7.49
606	Pte.	MARKEY John	C	-	Killed at Chilianwala
1377	Pte.	MARSHALL Edward	C	-	Killed at Chilianwala
1539	Pte.	MAYES Henry	C	-	Died 7.9.49
1185	Cpl.	MEADOWS George	C	G	Wounded at Chilianwala
1498	Pte.	MILLIGAN G. James	C	-	Killed at Chilianwala
1338	Cpl.	MOODY Thomas	C	G	Wounded 13.1.49
1884	Pte.	MUNDAY Peter	-	-	Died 10.5.49
1581	Pte.	NESTOR Patrick	C	G	Invalided 16.8.49 to England 7.2.50
1602	Pte.	NEWBERRY Francis	C	G	Wounded at Chilianwala
615	Pte.	NORTON Edward	C	-	Killed at Chilianwala
1659	Pte.	O'CONNOR Owen	C	G	Died 16.9.49
453	Cpl.	OGDEN Samuel	-	G	Died 4.6.49
1296	Sjt.	O'NEIL Charles H.	C	G	Wounded 22.11.48
676	Pte.	PAYNE Edward	C	G	Drowned 2.1.51
1679	Pte.	PELVIN James	C	G	Died 18.9.49
1358	Pte.	PICKERING John	C	G	Died 15.9.50
1685	Pte.	PILBEAM William	C	-	Killed at Chilianwala
738	T.S.M.	PILCHER James	C	G	Discharge by purchase 30.6.49
1522	Pte.	POTTER Henry	C	G	Wounded at Goojerat
1146	Pte.	REED Richard	C	-	Killed at Chilianwala
1523	Pte.	REGAN Owen	C	-	Killed at Chilianwala
1375	Pte.	REID William	C	G	Died 20.9.50

3rd Light Dragoons continued

1751	Pte.	REYNOLDS Floyd	C	G	Wounded at Chilianwala
1275	Pte.	RODMAN Henry	-	-	Died 20.12.48
1654	Pte.	SHAPLAND William	C	G	Died 15.7.50
990	Pte.	SHIELD Edward	C	G	Discharge by purchase 28.2.50
1304	T.S.M.	SINCOCK John	C	G	Died 22.12.50
1607	Pte.	SLADE James	C	-	Killed at Chilianwala
1036	Pte.	SMITH C. Edward	C	G	Discharge by purchase 31.1.51
1484	Pte.	SOPER Walter	C	G	Died 16.11.50
1641	Pte.	STEVENSON James	C	G	Invalided 24.8.49, England 7.2.50
1778	Pte.	STEWART Edwin	C	-	Drowned 14.3.49
850	Pte.	STONELY Randal	C	G	Invalided 20.10.49. Permitted to remain in India
1208	Pte.	STOTTER William	C	G	Wounded 3.12.48 Died 4.2.51
1652	Pte.	SWAN William	C	-	Killed at Chilianwala
1655	Pte.	TEALE John	C	-	Wounded at Chilianwala. Invalided 27.8.50 England 26.2.51
1505	Sjt.	THOMPSON Daniel	C	-	Killed at Chilianwala 13.1.49
1842	Pte.	THORNETT T. BRADLEY	C	G	Discharge by purchase 30.9.50
1173	Pte.	THYER James	C	-	Killed at Chilianwala
	Lieut.	TRAVERS J.H.	C	G	Died at sea 18.5.50
	Capt.	UNETT W.	C	G	Wounded at Chilianwala 13.1.49
1463	Pte.	UPTON William (1)	C	G	Wounded at Chilianwala
244	Sjt.	WALKER Thomas	-	G	Invalided 24.8.49 to England 7.2.50
1858	Pte.	WARD George	-	G	Died 11.10.49
1644	Pte.	WATTS William	C	G	Invalided 27.8.50, England 26.2.51
859	Pte.	WHITAKER John	C	G	Invalided 25.10.50 Permitted to remain in India
1240	Pte.	WILLIAMS Frederick	C	G	Discharge by purchase 30.11.50
744	Pte.	WITCHER John	-	-	Died 7.1.49

* * *

9th LANCERS

1016	Pte.	ABRAHAM Isaac	C	G	Died 25.6.49
782	Pte.	ADAMS Edward	C	G	Died 13.9.49
1584	Pte.	ALLCOCK Joseph	C	G	Died 6.10.49
1529	Pte.	AMPS John	C	G	Died 10.8.49
593	Pte.	BALLENTINE James	C	G	Died 27.6.50
988	Pte.	BECK Thomas	C	G	To England Free discharge 1.3.50
458	Pte.	BORREN Patrick	C	G	Died 18.3.49
1465	Pte.	BRANDRETH John	C	G	Died 2.5.49
1125	Pte.	BREEN Lother	C	G	Invalided to England 1.3.50
998	Pte.	BRITTLEBANK	-	G	Invalided to England 1.2.51
721	Pte.	BROWN David	C	G	Invalided to England 1.2.51
1412	Pte.	BROWNLESS William	C	G	Discharge by purchase 30.9.50
984	Pte.	BUDGEN William	C	G	Died 18.8.49
459	Pte.	BYRNE John	C	G	To England Free discharge 1.3.50
1127	Cpl.	CALCUTT Richard	C	-	Killed in Action at Chilianwala
1600	Pte.	CARLTON James	C	G	Died 25.1.51
1356	Pte.	CHAPMAN William	Medal Only		Invalided to England 1.2.51
1530	Sjt.	CLARK Alfred	C	G	Died 3.5.49

9th Lancers continued

1150	Pte.	CLARK David	Medal only		Died 26.12.48
1573	Pte.	CLARKE Alfred	C	G	Died 27.12.50
747	Pte.	CLARKE Joseph	C	G	Discharged by purchase 30.9.50
1274	Pte.	COATES Robert	C	G	Invalided to England 1.3.50
1199	Cpl.	COLLING William Henry	C	G	Discharged by purchase 20.10.49
1480	Pte.	CORFIELD John	Medal only		Died 9.1.49
1045	Pte.	CREASY Henry	C	G	Died 3.7.49
835	Pte.	CRITCHER Alfred	C	G	Died 10.3.51
772	Pte.	CUNNIAM John	C	-	Killed in action in Chilianwala
1577	Pte.	CURTIS William	C	G	Died 23.9.49
1098	Pte.	CUTTING George	C	G	Died
972	Pte.	DAINE John Cole	C	G	Died 30.12.49
453	Pte.	DALTON Robert	C	-	Killed in action at Chilianwala
1520	Pte.	DIVINE Patrick	C	G	Died 30.10.49
Apprentice		DIXON William	C	G	Joined from No.10 Light Field Artillery 22.1.49
310	Pte.	DONELAN Patrick	C	G	Died 13.7.49
951	Cpl.	DOLAN Patrick	C	G	Died 4.5.49
635	Pte.	DROUGHT George	C	G	Discharged by purchase 30.9.50
805	O.R.C.	DUCKER William F.	C	G	Embarked for England to join Depot 1.2.51
548	Pte.	DUNCAN James	C	G	Died 1.11.49
1589	Pte.	FELL Walter W.	C	G	Discharged by purchase 6.10.49
1394	Pte.	FISHER William Lowe	C	G	Died 15.9.49
1224	Pte.	FITZGERALD Patrick	C	G	Discharged with ignominy 13.4.50
441	Pte.	FOSTER James	C	G	Died 1.11.49
1015	Pte.	FRAM George	C	G	Died 27.6.49
1608	Pte.	FRENCH Henry	C	G	Died 10.3.49
1587	Pte.	FROST Samuel	-	G	To 3rd Light Dragoons 31.3.49
	Lt.Col.	FULLERTON James A.	Medal only		Died 28.4.50 at Cashmere
654	Sjt.	GAUDIN Henry	C	G	Discharged 31.5.51
1088	Pte.	GESSOP John	C	G	Died 1.12.49
1315	Pte.	GILLING James	C	G	Discharged by purchase 30.9.50
954	Pte.	GREENWOOD Bentley	C	G	Died 17.2.50
797	Pte.	GRIFFITHS	C	G	Died 12.4.49
1219	Pay.Mst.Sjt.	GRIFFITHS Telemachus P.	C	G	Discharged by purchase 13.10.49
1519	Pte.	GUY George John	C	G	Invalided to England 1.2.51
1593	Pte.	HARBER Frederick	C	G	Died 6.4.49
510	Sjt.	HARDIE John	-	G	Died 24.4.49
1415	Pte.	HARLING Charles	C	G	Died 19.10.49
1302	Pte.	HARRIS Robert	C	G	Discharged by purchase 30.9.50
1029	Pte.	HATCH Rowland	C	G	Invalided to England 1.2.51
1114	Pte.	HENDERSON Robert	C	G	Died 30.11.50
1244	Pte.	HODGETTS Joseph	C	G	Discharged by purchase 31.5.50
1005	Pte.	HOLDEN George	C	G	To 32nd Foot 31.3.51
463	Pte.	HORNE Wilbert	C	G	Died 2.12.49
1533	Pte.	HUTCHINGS Charles	C	G	Medal Forfeited
682	Pte.	INMAN Robert	C	-	Died 5.2.49
1272	Pte.	JACKSON George F.	C	G	Discharged by purchase 30.11.50
1062	Pte.	JOHNSON Thomas	C	G	Died 18.9.50

499	Pte.	JOHNSTON Thomas	C	G	Died 21.2.50
1074	Pte.	JORDAN Elias	C	G	Died 30.11.49
1121	Pte.	KELLY Patrick	C	G	Died 29.10.49
1053	Pte.	KEY William	C	G	Discharge by purchase 30.9.50
1167	Pte.	KNOWLES Robert	C	G	To England Free discharge 1.2.51
591	Pte.	LETTERS Bernard	C	G	Died 5.6.49
1466	Pte.	LIMBREY George	C	-	Died 22.1.49
880	Pte.	LITTLE Alfred J.	C	G	Died 19.5.50
781	Pte.	LOVELACE Francis	C	G	Died
1107	Trumpeter	McDONALD Edward	C	G	Died 9.6.49
970	Sjt.	McEWEN James	C	G	Invalided to England 1.3.50
1148	Troop Sjt/Maj.	McNAUGHTON Patrick	C	G	Died 12.4.49
506	Troop Sjt/Maj.	McNICOL Robert	C	G	Died 6.10.49
509	Sjt.	McQUEEN John	Medal only		Died 24.12.48
770	Pte.	McTEAGUE Thomas	C	G	Deserted
1570	Pte.	MADAGAN Dennis	-	G	Died 26.7.49
656	Pte.	MAGOVERAN Thomas	C	G	Died 31.5.50
1187	Trumpeter	MARRAY Robert	C	G	Died 31.3.49
1102	Pte.	MATTHEWS Abraham	C	-	Killed in Action at Chilianwala
1576	Pte.	MITCHINSON William	C	G	Died 16.10.50
1146	Pte.	MORLEY Henry	C	G	To England Free discharge 1.2.51
1436	Pte.	NAPIER John	C	G	Died 12.9.49
1341	Pte.	NEILAND John	C	G	Died 9.1.50
1393	Cpl.	NIGHTINGALE Frederick	C	G	Died 28.8.49
1522	Pte.	ORREN John	C	G	Died 27.7.50
918	Pte.	PALMER Robert Richard	C	G	Invalided to England 1.2.51
498	Pte.	PAYMEN Thomas	C	G	Invalided to England 1.2.51
1300	Pte.	PEIRCE George	C	G	Died 17.4.49
1540	Pte.	PENDREY Peter	C	G	Died 1.4.49
810	Pte.	POPCOCK George	C	G	Died 13.8.49
853	Pte.	PRESTON Peter	C	G	Died 27.7.50
794	Pte.	PROSSER William	C	G	Died 22.9.49
1211	Pte.	READ James	C	G	Died 3.11.49
1543	Pte.	REED Thomas	C	G	Died 11.10.49
1576	Pte.	RESTALL William	-	G	Died 7.9.49
950	Pte.	ROBINSON Robert	C	G	Died 14.8.49
1375	Pte.	SALLONE Thomas	C	G	Transported by Sentence of General Court Marshall 28.4.50
945	Pte.	SALTRY John	C	G	Died 11.10.49
1162	Pte.	SAVAGE William	C	G	Died 24.10.49
1331	Pte.	SCANLAN Timothy	C	G	Discharge by purchase 30.9.50
1010	Pte.	SELMAN Henry	C	G	Died 22.3.49
1173	Pte.	SLADE Thomas	C	G	To England Free discharge 1.2.51
1484	Pte.	SMITH James (2)	C	G	Died 6.7.49
704	Sjt.	SMITH Joseph	C	G	Died 16.7.50
615	Pte.	SMITH Stevenson	C	G	Died 28.6.49
907	Pte.	SMITH Thomas L.	C	G	Died 26.2.50

9th Lancers continued

Steward		SNOOK Thomas	C	G	Died 5.9.49
493	Sjt.	SOTHERAN William	C	G	Died 19.7.50
570	Pte.	STEER James	C	G	Discharge by purchase 28.2.51
983	Pte.	STEPHENS John	C	G	Died 5.10.49
1112	Pte.	STEWART Alexander	C	G	Died 30.4.50
1578	Pte.	SUTTON William (2)	C	G	Died 16.8.49
612	Pte.	SWEENEY James	C	G	To England Free discharge 1.2.51
1338	Pte.	THOMAS Robert	C	G	Died 14.4.49
1282	Pte.	THOMAS William	C	G	Died 18.12.50
1398	Cpl.	THOMPSON John	C	G	Died 2.8.49
1346	Pte.	THOMPSON John (1)	C	G	Died 21.6.49
534	Pte.	THOMSON William (1)	C	G	Died 19.3.49
1246	Pte.	TRANTER George	C	G	Discharge by purchase 30.9.50
361	Pte.	TUCKER William	-	G	Died 8.5.49
469 Troop Sjt.Maj.		VANTREIGHT Joseph	C	G	Died 14.11.49
923	Pte.	WADE Thomas	C	G	Died 7.9.49
901	Pte.	WALTER Lemon H.	C	G	Discharge by purchase 30.9.50
589	Pte.	WARD William	C	G	Died 24.2.50
1601	Pte.	WARE Henry	C	G	Died 17.6.50
1252	Pte.	WEBLEY Andrew	C	G	Died 12.5.49
1546	Pte.	WELLS Joseph	C	G	Died 24.7.50
473 Troop Sjt.Maj.		WILLIAMS John	C	G	Free discharge 30.11.50
1308	Pte.	WILLIAMS Henry	C	G	Discharge by purchase 30.9.50
1239	Pte.	WILLIAMS Thomas S.	C	G	Discharge by purchase 30.9.50
1316	Pte.	WOOD Robert	C	G	Discharge by purchase 30.9.50
401	Tmpt.Major	WOODWARD George	C	G	Invalided to England 1.2.51

* * *

14th LIGHT DRAGOONS

907	Pte.	ALDERTON John	-	-	Killed 22.11.48
1279	Sjt.	ALLISON William	C	G	Died 4.9.49
1219	Pte.	ALPIN William	-	-	Killed 22.11.48
503	Pte.	ANDREWS Joseph	C	G	Discharged with ignominy
775	Pte.	ATKIN Robert Charles	C	G	Died 26.5.51
867	Pte.	ATKINS George	C	-	Killed at Chilianwalla
692	Pte.	BAGG Richard	-	-	Killed 22.11.48
1276	Pte.	BARTON Alfred	C	G	Died 10.1.51
667	Pte.	BATEMAN John	C	G	Died 9.2.51
640	Pte.	BATTERSBEE John	C	G	Died 1.5.51
1150/858	Pte.	BEAR William	C	G	Died 22.10.49
886	Pte.	BELL John	C	G	Wounded 21.2.49
924	Pte.	BENETT James	C	G	Died 11.9.49
Qr.Master		BENNETT Thomas	C	G	Wounded 22.11.48
637	Cpl.	BEST George	C	G	Wounded 22.11.48 Invalided 9.2.49 to England 10.5.49
952	Pte.	BOSWELL Thomas Tippin	C	G	Invalided 26.8.50, England 1.2.51
1452	Pte.	BRAISBY William	C	G	Wounded at Chilianwala
1351	Pte.	BRAZENOR William	-	-	Killed 22.11.48
1429	Pte.	BRICK Timothy	C	G	Died

1511	Pte.	BROWN Isaac	C	G	Died 21.5.49
331	Pte.	BROWN Robert	C	G	Died 22.12.50
1193	Pte.	BROWN Stephen	C	G	Discharged
466	Pte.	BYRNE Edward	C	-	Died 15.8.49
1323	Pte.	BYRNE Patrick	C	G	Wounded 22.11.48
686	Pte.	CARPENTER Arthur	C	-	Died 14.2.49
795	Sjt.	CARREY William E.	C	G	Discharged by purchase 2.4.50
875	Pte.	CATO Henry	C	G	Wounded at Chilianwala
962/1101	Pte.	CHAMBERLAIN John	C	G	Sentenced to 7 years transportation
2685/1450	Pte.	CHEETHAM Isaac	C	G	Wounded 22.11.48
1331	Pte.	CLIFFORD John	C	G	Died
1177	Pte.	CLIFTON James	C	G	Wounded 22.11.48
715	Pte.	COTTRILL Thomas	C	G	Reduced from Armoured Serjeant
983/1124	Pay.Mst.St.	CROOT John	C	G	Died 5.8.50
1158	Sjt.	CROUCHER Alfred	C	G	Died 14.4.50
	Lieut.	CURETON Augustus John	C	-	Killed at Chilianwala
1483	Pte.	DADSON John	C	G	Wounded at Chilianwala
1434	Pte.	DARGE Joseph	C	G	Died 5.12.50
407/1050	Pte.	DAVIS William	C	G	Invalided 26.8.50, to England 1.2.51
1488	Pte.	DUNFORD George	C	G	Died 13.7.50
1342	Pte.	DUNKERTON William	C	G	Wounded 22.11.48
1082/1138	Pte.	DUNN Joseph	-	-	Died 25.10.50
947	Pte.	DYAS Edward	C	G	Died 12.2.51
841	Pte.	EAST Thomas	-	-	Died
835	Pte.	EAVNS David	C	-	Killed at Chilianwala
659	Pte.	FAIRHEAD Tyrrell	C	G	Died 5.6.50
273	Sjt.	FEELEY William	-	-	Invalided 21.8.49, to England 16.2.50
609	Pte.	FELLS Frederick	C	G	Wounded 22.11.48
	Capt.	FITZGERALD John Foster	-	-	Wounded 22.11.48, Died of wounds 26.11.48
1487	Pte.	FOSTER John	-	-	Died 21.12.50
1440	Pte.	FOX Charles	-	-	Killed 22.11.48
402/932	Pte.	FRAZER William	C	G	Wounded at Chilianwala
727	Cpl.	FULWELL Henry	C	G	Wounded 22.11.48
1202	Pte.	FURNESS George	C	G	Died 9.2.50
	Capt.	GALL Richard Herbert	C	G	Wounded 22.11.48
939/612	Pte.	GARDNER James	C	G	Reduced from T.S.M. 7.5.50
1412	Pte.	GIBSON James	C	G	Died 20.7.49
	Major	GODDARD John Hesketh	C	G	Wounded at Goojerat
1208	Pte.	GOLDRIDGE George	C	G	Resigned Trumpeter 21.3.51
1149	Sjt.	GOOCH Thomas	C	-	Wounded 31.3.49, Invalided 9.2.49, to England 10.5.49
1245/1368	Pte.	GOOD Thomas	C	G	Wounded 22.11.48
508/941	Pte.	GREEN James	C	G	Died 19.3.51
712	Sch.Mst.Sjt.	HANLEY Frederick	-	-	Died 19.2.49
417	Sjt.	HARWOOD John	-	-	Wounded 22.11.48, Inavlided 9.2.49, to England 10.5.49

367	Pte.	HATTON John	-	-	Killed 22.11.48
	Lt.Col.	HAVELOCK William KH	-	-	Killed in Action 22.11.48
1435	Pte.	HAWKER Richard	C	G	Died 26.2.49
300	Pte.	HAYWARD John	C	G	Wounded 22.11.48
431/636	Pte.	HEIFFERNAN Richard	C	-	Died 26.2.49
1401	Pte.	HEMMINGS Henry	-	-	Died 4.8.49
1502	Pte.	HOGG David	C	G	Wounded 21.2.49
542	Sjt.	HOLMES John	C	G	Died 10.11.50
1521	Pte.	HOPKINS Joseph	C	G	Discharge by purchase 10.6.50
590/1085	Pte.	HORNE Henry	C	G	Died 2.6.50
1428	Pte.	HUNGERFORD Richard	-	-	Killed 22.11.48
1239	Pte.	HUTTON James	-	-	Reduced from Serjeant 31.8.49,Died 3.9.49
1260	Pte.	JACOB Gabriel Fred.Wm.	C	G	Wounded at Chilianwala,Discharged by purchase 26.4.50
791	Pte.	JENNINGS Benjamin	-	-	Died of wounds 23.11.48 received on 22.11.48
1326	Cpl.	JOHNSON Benjamin	-	-	Died 8.6.49
1398	Pte.	JOLLY Josiah	C	G	Died 9.12.49
1229	Pte.	JONES Thomas Charles	C	G	Invalided 26.8.50, England 1.2.51
389/1046	Pte.	KAVANAGH Nicholas	C	G	Invalided 26.8.50, England 1.2.51
816	Pte.	KELLY John	C	G	Discharge by purchase 12.11.50
510/1069	Pte.	KING Michael	-	-	Invalided 21.8.49, England 16.2.50
552	Pte.	KING Thomas	C	G	Invalided 21.8.49, England 16.2.50
877	Cpl.	LADE John	C	G	Died 4.1.51
975	Cpl.	LAMB Peter	C	G	Died 27.7.49
1396	Pte.	LATTER James	C	G	Died 18.10.50
221	Pte.	LEE William	C	G	Reduced from Trumpeter Major 15.4.50
986	Pte.	LEE William	C	G	Wounded at Chilianwala - Died.
961	Cpl.	LEIGH John	C	G	Wounded 22.11.28
1074/1136	Pte.	LLEWELLEN Thomas	C	G	Died 2.3.51
	Lieut.	LLOYD Ambrose	C	G	Killed at Goojerat
929	Sjt.	MADDERS James	C	G	Died 16.11.49
543	T.S.M.	MATTHEWS John	C	G	Died 24.1.50
1468	Pte.	MAY Henry	C	G	Died 4.11.50
1178	Pte.	McCORMACK Wilson	C	G	Discharge by purchase 27.6.49
467/1061	Pte.	McDERMOT James	-	-	Died 25.6.49
1215	Pte.	McDONALD Henry	C	G	Died 23.8.49
	Lieut.	McMAHON William	C	G	Wounded 22.11.48
1245	Pte.	MERAC Theophilus	-	-	Died 2.12.48
1656/ 2916/1547	Pte.	MILES Ambrose	C	-	Wounded 22.11.48, invalided 21.8.49, England 16.2.50
921	Pte.	MILES Henry	C	G	Died
732	Sjt.	MILES Thomas	-	-	Died 20.1.49
960	Pte.	MILLER John	C	G	Died 6.6.50
1541	Pte.	MILLS Daniel	C	G	Invalided 26.8.50, England 1.2.51
479	Pte.	MORRIN Daniel	C	-	Wounded at Chilianwala, invalided 9.2.49, to England 10.5.49
567	Pte.	MORRIS William	C	-	Wounded 22.11.48

14th Light Dragoons continued

No.	Rank	Name			Remarks
795/1083	Pte.	MURDIX William	-	-	Wounded 22.11.48, invalided 9.2.49, to England 10.5.49
1143	Pte.	MURRAY Patrick	C	G	Transfered 22nd Foot 1.10.50, duplicate issued 22.5.56
413	Pte.	NASH William	-	-	Died 20.12.48
	Lieut.	NEED Arthur	-	G	and Mooltan Bar
820	Pte.	NISBET John	C	G	Died 18.4.49
615/1089	Pte.	OCKFORD Henry	C	G	Died 4.6.50
1234	Pte.	OTHEN Charles	-	-	Died 20.11.48
1524	Pte.	PENDRY Shadrack	C	G	Died 9.6.49
1385	Pte.	RENN William	C	G	Died 11.5.51
848	Pte.	PITT William	C	G	Wounded at Chilianwala
990	Pte.	POWER James	C	G	Discharge by purchase 1.4.50
973	Pte.	PRICE Charles	C	G	Died 13.9.50
1714/1366	Pte.	PRICE Jeremiah	C	G	Died 18.8.49
1479	Pte.	PRIDE Albert	C	G	Wounded at Goojerat
811	Pte.	RAINES James	-	-	Killed 22.11.48
950	Pte.	REED Chrales	C	-	Wounded 22.11.48, invalided 21.8.49, to England 16.2.50
685	Sjt.	REEVES Henry	-	-	Died 15.5.49
390/1047	Pte.	RICE Joseph	C	G	Invalided 26.8.50, England 1.2.51
314	Pte.	RILEY William	C	G	Wounded 22.11.48, Died 23.10.50
1433	Pte.	ROBERTS Richard	C	G	Died 22.12.50
703	Pte.	ROBERTSON Charles	C	G	Died
1210	Sjt.	ROBINSON Albert	C	G	Died 23.8.50
289	Pte.	ROBINSON Mark	C	G	Invalided 26.8.50, England 1.2.51
971	Pte.	ROGERS Henry	C	G	Hung himself (insane) 4.8.50
1405	Pte.	ROWLAND John	C	G	Wounded 22.11.48
726	Pte.	SARGENT Jacob	C	G	Died 1.6.49
	Capt.	SCUDAMORE Arthur	C	G	Wounded at Goojerat
895	Pte.	SEDGEWICK William	C	-	Wounded at Chilianwala
1172	Pte.	SENDELS Thomas	-	-	Died 8.11.48
1334	Cpl.	SEXTON George	C	G	Died 7.8.49
1517	Pte.	SEYMOUR Alfred	-	-	Died 23.11.48
1312	Pte.	SIMMONDS Jacob	C	G	Wounded 22.11.48
	Qr.Mst.	SHENTON George	C	G	Died at sea 2.3.50
893	Pte.	SHEPHERD John William	C	G	Died 8.10.49
850	Pte.	SMITH Benjamin	C	G	Wounded 22.11.48, invalided 26.8.50, to England 1.2.51
569	Pte.	SMITH John	C	G	Wounded at Chilianwala
699	Cpl.	SNOW Charles	-	-	Died 8.12.48
799	Pte.	STEAD Henry	C	G	Died 26.5.51
991	Pte.	STEELE Robert	C	G	Wounded at Chilianwala - Discharged.
	Lt.Col.	STEUART Charles	C	G	Wounded at Chilianwala
577	Cpl.	STORRIE John	C	G	Died 19.6.50
915	Pte.	SOUTHGATE James	C	G	Wounded at Chilianwala
1374	Pte.	THROSSELL Thomas	C	G	Died 21.8.50

14th Light Dragoons continued

1375	Cpl.	TODD William Parker	-	-	Killed 22.11.48
1441	Pte.	TOOKEY George	C	-	Killed at Chilianwala
1251	Sjt.	TRESS George	-	-	Died
1317	Pte.	TUTTELL Charles	-	-	Killed 22.11.48
1095/1142	Tptr.	VINCENT Richard	C	G	Died 15.3.50
1265	Cpl.	VINCENT Thomas Mulso	C	-	Wounded 22.11.48
	Lt.Col.	WALLACE-KING John CB	C	G	Shot himself 4.7.50
916/1118	Pte.	WALSH Arthur	-	-	Died 26.3.49
1406	Pte.	WARD John	-	-	Killed 22.11.48
731	Pte.	WARREN William	C	G	Reduced from Serjeant 23.8.50
890	Pte.	WEST James	C	G	Discharged
1157	Pte.	WHEELER Frederick Wm.	C	G	Died 15.9.49
844	Pte.	WILLIAMS George	-	-	Killed 22.11.48
1303	Pte.	WILLIAMS John Henry	C	G	Duplicate medal issued
777/1360	Pte.	WILLIS Samuel	C	G	Invalided 21.8.49, England 16.2.50
683/1095	Pte.	WILSON Thomas	C	G	Wounded at Goojerat, reduced from Corporal 26.2.50
1051/1133	Pte.	WISE Thomas	C	G	Sentenced to 7 years transportation
550	Pte.	WOOLGAR Charles	C	G	Died 15.3.50

* * *

10th FOOT

2243	Pte.	AHERN John	M	-	Sick proceeded to Feroze Pore 16.12.48
2296	Pte.	ALEXANDER James	M	-	Died of Wounds 17.11.48
1788	Pte.	ALLEN Robert	M	-	Sick to Feroze Pore 16.12.48 invalided to England 1.2.51
974	Pte.	ALLEN Thomas	M	G	Died 31.5.49
2294	Pte.	ALLEN Thomas	M	-	Killed in Action 9.9.48
654	Col.Sjt.	ALLEN William	M	G	Invalided to England 1.2.51
2056	Pte.	ANTHONY Michael	M	G	Invalided to England 1.3.50
1834	Pte.	ARMSTRONG Arthur	M	G	Died 27.10.50
1929	Cpl.	ARMSTRONG Joesph	M	-	Wounded 22.1.49 Left sick at Mooltan
640	Pte.	ARMSTRONG Thomas	M	G	Invalided to England 1.3.50
1586	Pte.	BAILEY Joseph	M	-	Sick, to Ferozepore 16.12.48
1514	Pte.	BAIRD William	M	-	Died of Wounds 23.2.48
1639	Pte.	BARFOOT George	M	-	Died of Wounds 10.9.48
2297	Pte.	BAYLEY James	M	G	Died 17.10.50
603	Pte.	BEARMAN Abraham	-	G	Invalided to England 1.3.50
631	Pte.	BENNETT Standish O.G.	M	G	Invalided to England 1.3.50
2189	Pte.	BERGIN Edward	M	-	Died 3.2.49
1730	Pte.	BISHOP John	M	-	Died 2.2.49
1166	Pte.	BLACKBURN Joesph	M	G	Invalided to England 1.2.51
Ensign		BLUETT W.H.P.G.	M	G	Joined Regt. 9.1.49
2236	Pte.	BOURKE Michael (2)	M	-	Wounded at Mooltan, invalided 1.3.50
1431	Pte.	BOWLER Timothy	M	-	Wounded at Mooltan, to England 10.5.49
2267	Pte.	BOWLER Thomas	M	-	Left sick at Mooltan, invalided 1.2.51

780	Pte.	BOYLE Charles	M	G	Invalided to England 1.2.51
750	Pte.	BOYLE Janes	M	G	Invalided to England 27.2.51
2283	Pte.	BOYLE Philip	M	G	Died 31.7.50
1677	Pte.	BRADSHAW Edwin	M	-	Left sick at Mooltan
1985	Pte.	BRADY James	M	G	Discharged 6.4.50
2210	Pte.	BRIER Martin	M	-	Wounded at Mooltan, invalided 1.3.50
1901	Pte.	BRIGGS George	M	-	Wounded at Mooltan, invalided 10.5.49
2005	Pte.	BRIGGS James M.	M	-	Left sick at Mooltan
1640	Pte.	BROKER Thomas	M	-	Died of Wounds 12.9.48
2388	Pte.	BROWN George	M	-	Died 28.11.48
2083	Pte.	BROWN James	M	G	Died 27.3.49
1986	Pte.	BROWNSELL James	M	G	Died 30.10.50
2412	Pte.	BURKE Henry	M	-	Killed in Action 9.9.48
2166	Pte.	BURKE Michael	M	-	Left sick at Mooltan
2107	Pte.	BURKE Patrick	M	-	Sick to Ferozepore 16.12.48, invalided to England 10.5.49
2302	Pte.	BURNS John	M	-	Died 19.2.48
2303	Pte.	BURTON Thomas	M	G	Died 11.11.49
2304	Pte.	BUTLER Pierce	M	G	Died 30.3.51
1475	Pte.	BUTLER Richard	M	-	Left at Ramnuggar Died 4.7.50
1348	Pte.	BYRNE John (1)	M	-	Died 16.8.48
1850	Pte.	BYRNE Patrick (2)	M	-	Wounded to Feroze 16.12.48
1943	Pte.	BYRNE Thomas (2)	M	-	Wounded at Mooltan, invalided 25.1.50
2106	Pte.	BYRNE Thomas (3)	M	-	Died 28.12.48
1548	Pte.	BYRNES Richard	M	-	Killed in Action 12.9.48
1873	Pte.	CALACKY Humphrey	M	-	Died 12.9.48
2030	Pte.	CAMPBELL John	M	G	Invalided to England 1.2.51
2244	Pte.	CAMPBELL John	-	-	Died 20.8.48
1488	Pte.	CAMPBELL Michael	M	G	Wounded 21.2.49, invalided 1.3.50
1674	Pte.	CARBURY James	-	-	Died 21.8.48
2523	Pte.	CARRIN Thomas	-	G	Died 3.5.50
1754	Pte.	CARTER Charles	M	-	Left sick at Mooltan
1923	Pte.	CARTWRIGHT Charles	M	G	Died 11.4.51
1300	Pte.	CAWLEY George	M	G	Died 28.7.49
2414	Pte.	CHAPMAN Robert	-	-	Died 29.8.48
1486	Pte.	CLANCY James	M	G	Died 3.1.51
1129	Pte.	CLYNES Patrick	M	G	Wounded 21.2.49, invalided 1.3.50
894	Cpl.	CODD James	M	-	Died of Wounds 11.10.48
2164	Pte.	COMERFORD Michael	M	G	Died 7.4.50
2282	Pte.	CONDON Patrick	M	G	Invalided to England 1.2.51
1658	Pte.	CONNOLLY John	M	G	Died 22.3.50
1934	Pte.	CONWAY James	M	-	Wounded 7.11.48, invalided 1.3.50
2063	Pte.	COOPER James	M	G	Invalided to England 1.2.51
2417	Pte.	CORCORAN Charles	M	-	Killed in Action 13.9.48
2010	Sjt.	COSGRAVE James	M	-	Left sick at Ramnuggar
2418	Pte.	COSTELLO Charles	-	-	Died 10.8.48
1047	Pte.	COX Richard	M	-	Sick, proceeded to Feroze 16.12.48
2318	Pte.	CREAMEOR Patrick (1)	M	-	Died of Wounds 16.11.48

1275	Pte.	CREAMEOR Patrick (2)	M	G	Died 26.7.51
582	Pte.	CUNNINGHAM James	M	G	Wounded, invalided 1.3.50
623	Pte.	CURTIN Michael	M	G	Invalided to England 1.2.51
2062	Pte.	CUSH John	M	-	Died 23.4.49
1632	Clr.Sjt.	CUTHBERTSON Stephen	M	G	Died 4.10.49
1039	Pte.	DAILEY Michael	M	G	Invalided to England 1.2.51
2108	Pte.	DALTON James	M	G	Invalided to England 1.3.50
2286	Pte.	DALTON John	M	-	Left sick at Mooltan, died 20.2.49
1383	Pte.	DAVIES George	-	G	Killed in Action 21.2.49
1649	Pte.	DAVIES Richard	M	-	Died 23.9.48
1779	Pte.	DAVIES Thomas (2)	M	G	Died 10.7.50
2067	Pte.	DAWSON William	M	-	Died 18.11.48
2227	Pte.	DAY James	-	-	Died 27.8.48
2307	Pte.	DELANEY Patrick	M	-	Left sick at Ramnuggar, died 23.12.49
773	Pte.	DELAP Samuel	M	G	Invalided to England 1.3.50
1956	Pte.	DEMPSEY Denis (1)	M	G	Died 28.10.49
1678	Cpl.	DENBIGH Thomas W.	M	-	Died Dysentry 31.1.49
1153	Pte.	DEWHURST William	M	-	Killed in Action 12.9.48
1015	Cpl.	DISKIN Patrick	M	-	Died 16.11.48
2246	Pte.	DONLIN William	M	-	Died of Wounds 24.1.49
2121	Pte.	DONOVAN Patrick	M	-	Died of Wounds 6.11.48
1940	Pte.	DOOLEY John	M	G	Died 5.3.50
2421	Pte.	DOWN John	M	-	Wounded at Mooltan, invalided 11.3.50
2045	Pte.	DRENNAN Patrick	M	G	Left sick at Mooltan
906	Pte.	DRISCOLL Patrick	M	-	Sick to Feroze 16.12.48, to England 1.2.51
2488	Pte.	DUFF William	-	G	Died 31.8.50
1062	Pte.	DUNNE Thomas	M	G	Discharged 1.5.50
1360	Pte.	DWYRE John	M	-	Wounded at Mooltan, invalided 1.3.50
2257	Pte.	DWYRE John	M	-	Wounded, left sick at Mooltan, to England 1.8.50
2084	Pte.	EGAN Michael	M	G	Died 27.3.50
1086	Pte.	ENGLISH John	M	G	Died 2.9.51
2262	Pte.	FALVEY Daniel	M	-	Wounded left at Mooltan, to England 1.2.51
2314	Pte.	FARRELL James	M	G	Died 16.6.51
1821	.Pte.	FENTON James	M	-	Died 21.12.48
1490	Pte.	FERGUSON John (1)	-	-	Died 26.8.48
1240	Pte.	FERRIS Thomas	M	-	Died 13.1.49
976	Pte.	FISK John	M	-	Left sick at Ramnuggar
2285	Pte.	FITTON Richard	M	-	Sick to Ferozepore 16.12.48, died 19.10.50
2317	Pte.	FITZGERALD Richard	M	G	Died 5.4.51
1435	Pte.	FLANAGAN Thomas	M	G	Died 11.11.50
2321	Pte.	FLYNN James	M	-	Sick to Ferozepore 16.12.48
2228	Pte.	FOSTER Benjamin	-	G	Discharde 10.5.50
2090	Pte.	FRANCIS Jacob	M	G	Died 1.10.50
2039	Pte.	GAFFNEY James	-	-	Died 15.8.48
2239	Pte.	GALLAHER James	M	-	Left sick at Ramnuggar
	Lieut.	GALLOWAY S.C.C.	M	G	Died of Wounds 16.7.50

1516	Pte.	GILKINSON William	M	G	Died 9.4.51
1229	Pte.	GLYNN Patrick	M	G	Transerred to 94th Foot 1.8.49
	Ensign	GOODFELLOW Joseph	M	-	Promoted Lieutenant 24th Foot 14.1.49
901	Pte.	GRADY Lawrence	M	-	Left sick at Ramnuggar
1128	Pte.	GRANT Thomas	-	G	Invalided to England 27.2.50
1604	Pte.	GREEN William	M	-	Wounded at Mooltan, invalided 1.3.50
1391	Pte.	GREGORY Thomas	M	-	Killed in Action 9.9.48
1670	Pte.	GRICE James	-	-	Invalided to England 9.2.49
2247	Pte.	GRIFFIN John	M	-	Wounded 9.9.48, invalided 10.5.49
1653	Pte.	GRIFFITHS Edward	M	-	Died of Wounds 10.9.48
2205	Pte.	GRIGGS James	M	-	Sick, died 17.12.49
2328	Pte.	HALLORAN Michael	M	G	Died 5.10.49
2433	Pte.	HALLORAN William	M	G	To 98th Foot
785	Pte.	HANNAR William	M	-	Invalided to England 1.3.50
558	Pte.	HARRIGAN James	M	G	Died 15.6.49
2434	Pte.	HARRIS James	M	G	Died 12.9.49
1593	Pte.	HATTON Charles	M	G	Died 22.11.49
1174	Pte.	HAYES Patrick	M	-	Wounded at Mooltan, invalided 25.1.50
1961	Pte.	HENRY James	M	G	Discharged 20.8.50
1523	Pte.	HILL Ambrose	M	-	Left sick at Ramnuggar, to England 1.3.50
2538	Pte.	HODGES Terence	-	G	Died 6.11.50
	Capt.	HOLLINSWORTH H.A.	M	-	Died of Wounds 3.10.48
	Lieut.	HERBERT J.S.	M	-	Died of Wounds 17.2.49
2233	Pte.	HONNOR Ashton	M	-	Left sick at Mooltan
869	Pte.	HORAN John	M	-	Died of Wounds 28.12.48
2436	Pte.	HORNE Joseph	M	G	Invalided to England 1.3.50
1311	Pte.	HORROCKS John	M	-	Died Dysentry 30.11.48
2183	Pte.	HOWMAN George	M	G	Invalided to England 1.2.51
2437	Pte.	HOWARD William	M	-	Wounded at Mooltan, invalided 1.2.51
1156	Pte.	HUBBARD William	M	G	Died 20.1.51
1880	Pte.	HUGHES John (1)	M	-	Left sick at Mooltan
2069	Pte.	HUGHES John	M	G	Invalided to England 1.2.51
964	Pte.	HUNT James	M	-	Wounded at Mooltan, discharged Calcutta 13.2.50
1294	Pte.	HUNT Samuel	M	-	Left sick at Ramnuggar, died 14.6.50
2160	Pte.	HURLEY Michael	M	-	Killed in Action 9.9.48
2475	Pte.	HUXLEY Ebenezer	M	G	Died 18.6.50
2335	Pte.	HUXLEY Thomas	M	-	Sick to Feroze 16/12/48
1939	Pte.	HYLAND James	M	-	Left sick at Ramnuggar
789	Clr.Sjt.	HYNES Francis	-	-	Died 27.8.48
1584	Pte.	JONES Thomas	M	-	Died 10.10.48
2293	Pte.	KEANE Thomas	M	-	Left Sick at Mooltan
1990	Pte.	KEATING Peter	M	-	Died of Wounds 13.10.48
1738	Pte.	KEEFE John (1)	M	G	Died 18.11.50
1881	Pte.	KENYON Francis	M	G	Died 18.7.49
1396	Pte.	KENYON James	M	G	Killed in Action 21.2.49
2000	Pte.	KEYBURN Robert	M	-	Left sick at Ramnuggar
2109	Pte.	KITCHING Joshua	M	-	Wounded at Mooltan, to England 1.3.50

10th Foot continued

1857	Pte.	LACEY Robert	M	G	Died 7.11.50
1645	Pte.	LAGGIN Bernard	-	-	Died 29.8.48
2524	Pte.	LAMPHIER Michael	-	-	Left sick at Ramnuggar 17.2.49
2100	Pte.	LARNEY Bernard	M	-	Killed in Action 9.9.48
1323	Pte.	LAWLOR Christopher	M	-	Died 26.9.48
2264	Pte.	LAWLOR Patrick	M	G	Died of Wounds 23.3.49
2248	Pte.	LAWLOR Richard	M	-	Wounded at Mooltan, invalided 1.3.50
605	Dmr.	LAYO Edmund	-	G	Invalided 1.3.50
813	Cpl.	LEGGATT Edward	M	-	Wounded 9.9.48, invalided to England 10.5.49
2272	Cpl.	LLOYD William	M	G	Died Dysentry 13.1.50
	Capt.	LONGDEN H.E.	M	G	Staff Employment Mooltan Field Force
1249	Pte.	LYON Jonathan	M	-	Left sick at Mooltan
1048	Pte.	MADDIGAN Patrick	M	-	Wounded at Mooltan
2346	Pte.	MAGAR Thomas	M	G	To 29th Foot 9.8.49
853	Pte.	MAHER Patrick	M	G	Died 12.5.50
1530	Pte.	MAHON John	M	G	Invalided to England 1.2.51
2215	Pte.	MAHONEY Miles	M	-	Sick, invalided to England 10.5.49
1241	Pte.	MALLON Owen	M	-	Wounded at Mooltan
2141	Pte.	MALONE Philip	M	G	To 2nd Bengal European Regt.
1139	Pte.	MALONEY Daniel	M	-	Left sick at Mooltan
2098	Pte.	MALONEY Michael	-	-	Left sick at Ramnuggar
1057	Cpl.	MANION John	M	G	Died 7.9.50
1672	Pte.	MARSH George	M	-	Sick to England 1.3.50
672	Cpl.	MASON George	M	G	Killed in Action 21.2.49
1636	Pte.	MATSON William	M	-	Left sick at Mooltan
1671	Pte.	MATTHEWS Henry	M	G	Wounded 21.2.49, to England 1.3.50
778	Pte.	MEBERY Thomas	M	G	Invalided to England 1.2.51
1270	Cpl.	MEREDITH John	M	-	Wounded 12.9.48, invalided to England 1.2.51
1895	Pte.	MILLER Joseph	M	G	Discharge 12.6.50
	Major	MILLER Thomas	M	G	To 81st Foot 3.9.50
783	Pte.	MITCHELL David	M	-	Left sick at Mooltan
	Surgeon	MOCKLET Edward	M	G	Absent without leave from 31.5.51
	Major	MONTIZAMBERT G.S.	M	-	Killed in Action 12.9.48
	Capt.	MOORE G.F.	M	-	Wounded 4.11.48
580	Pte.	MORAN Christopher	M	G	Invalided to England 1.3.50
2289	Pte.	MORIARTY Cornelius	M	-	Killed at Mooltan 6.1.49
2113	Pte.	MORRIS Patrick	M	-	Left sick at Ramnuggar, to England 1.3.50
2050	Pte.	MORRISSEY Patrick	M	G	Invalided to England 1.2.51
2106	Pte.	MORRISSEY Thomas	M	G	Died 5.11.50
1724	Pte.	MULLIGAN Peter	M	G	Died 14.10.50
1614	Pte.	MURDOCK William	-	-	Died 27.8.48
1163	Pte.	MYERS John	M	-	Left sick at Ramnuggar, to England 1.3.50
2349	Pte.	McAULIFFE John	M	G	Killed in Action 21.2.49
2554	Pte.	McAULIFFE Patrick	-	G	Died 25.12.49
1767	Pte.	McCABE Hugh	M	G	Wounded 21.2.49, to England 12.3.51
1796	Pte.	McCABE John	M	G	Invalided to England 1.2.51
2385	Pte.	McCANN James (1)	M	-	Left sick at Mooltan

2353	Pte.	McCARRA Hurbert	M	-	Sick, died 24.4.49
1449	Pte.	McCARTHY Jeremiah (2)	M	G	Died 27.9.49
1545	Pte.	McCONNELL James	M	-	Died 30.12.48
2241	Pte.	McCOY William	M	-	Killed in Action 12.9.48
1957	Pte.	McDERMOTT William	M	-	Sick to Feroze 16.12.48
2249	Pte.	McDONALD Hugh	M	-	Left sick at Mooltan, died 10.5.51
2195	Pte.	McDONALD Thomas	M	-	Wounded. Taken prisoner 9.9.48, invalided to England 10.5.49
657	Pte.	McEVOY Henry	M	G	Invalided to England 1.3.50
1624	Pte.	McGEE Peter	M	G	Wounded 21.2.49, to England 1.3.50
1701	Pte.	McGEE Patrick	M	G	Died 13.3.49
2123	Pte.	McGRATH John	-	-	Invalided to England 9.2.49
	Capt.	McGREGOR Malcolm	M	-	Wounded 12.9.48
1969	Pte.	McGUIRE Martin	M	-	Died of Wounds 15.10.48
1429	Pte.	McKAY John	M	G	Dead
1466	Pte.	McLEAN Ebenezer	M	-	Killed in Action 27.9.48
1464	Sjt.	McMILLEN Phillip	M	-	Wounded 9.8.48, invalided to England 10.5.49
2072	Pte.	McMULLEN James	M	G	Invalided to England 1.2.51
2099	Pte.	McNALLY Peter	M	G	Invalided to England 1.2.51
1702	Pte.	McTAGUE Peter	M	G	Died 25.10.50
1505	Pte.	McWILLIAMS John	M	G	Left sick at Mooltan
2173	Pte.	NAILOR William	M	-	Sick, ot Feroze 16.12.48
969	Pte.	NASH Thomas	M	G	Died 23.10.49
1971	Pte.	NESTOR Edward	M	G	Died 26.11.50
2073	Pte.	O'BRIEN George	M	G	Wounded, to England 1.3.50
2074	Pte.	O'BRIEN Owen	M	-	Wounded at Mooltan, to England 10.5.49
1704	Pte.	O'DARE James	M	-	Left sick at Mooltan, died 17.6.49
1974	Pte.	O'DONNELL William	M	-	Sick, to England 25.1.50
879	Sjt.Maj.	O'DONNELL M.	M	G	Promoted Ensign 29.11.50
1080	Sjt.	O'DONNELL Michael	M	G	Died 9.9.51
1613	Pte.	O'HARE John (2)	M	-	Died at Mooltan 26.1.49
552	Pte.	ORPIN George	M	-	Sick to England 25.1.50
2128	Pte.	OVER William	M	-	Wounded left at Mooltan, to England 10.5.49
1567	Pte.	OWEN John	M	-	Died of Wounds 12.9.48
1844	Pte.	PASSINGTON James	M	G	Died 27.5.49
1312	Pte.	PEARSON Thomas	M	-	Left sick at Ramnuggar, to England 1.3.50
2266	Pte.	PHILLIPS Samuel	M	G	Died 12.8.51
626	Sjt.	PHILLIPS William	M	G	Died 8.10.50
2274	Pte.	PICKETT Frederick	M	G	Died 27.9.50
2176	Pte.	PLATTEN	M	-	Sick, to Feroze 16.12.48
719	Pte.	PRENDIVILLE Richard	M	-	Killed in Action 27.12.48
1570	Pte.	PRICE Thomas	M	-	Left sick at Mooltan, to England 1.3.50
1132	Pte.	QUILETR William	M	G	Discharge 10.6.50
2139	Pte.	QUINN Timothy	M	-	Wounded, Died 22.3.49
1397	Pte.	QUIRK Fenton	M	-	Left sick at Ramnuggar 17.2.49
1216	Pte.	QUISHEON Thomas	M	-	Invalided to England 10.5.49
1266	Pte.	READER William	M	G	Died 12.9.50

1753	Pte.	RIELLY James	M	-	Died 27.9.48
1626	Sjt.	REILLY John	M	G	Died 10.10.50
2489	Pte.	RILEY Henry	-	G	Died 4.8.49
1503	Pte.	RILEY James	M	G	Died 7.10.50
1204	Pte.	RIMMER James	M	G	Transferred to 98th Foot
821	Pte.	ROACHE William	M	-	Wounded at Mooltan, to England 1.2.51
1191	Sjt.	ROBERTS Edmund	M	G	Died 28.8.50
2378	Pte.	ROSSNEY John	M	G	Executed 28.7.51
1664	Pte.	ROWLANDS William	M	G	Invalided to England 1.3.50
600 Hos.Sjt.		RUSHMAN J.	-	G	Invalided to England 1.2.51
946	Pte.	RUSSELL John	M	G	Discharge to England 24.12.49
539	Pte.	RYAN Patrick	-	G	To England 1.3.50
	Capt.	SALL H.M.	M	G	Exchanged to 37th Foot 11.5.49
445	Pte.	SCANLON John	-	G	Invalided to England 1.3.50
1330	Pte.	SCHOFILED John	M	-	Wounded, left at Mooltan
1928	Pte.	SCOTT John	M	-	Sick, to Freoze 16.12.48
2218	Pte.	SCOTT Patrick	-	G	Invalided to England 1.3.50
2456	Pte.	SCULLY John	M	-	Invalided to England 1.3.50
2525	Pte.	SEARS John	-	G	Died 29.7.50
1571	Pte.	SELVES John	M	G	Invalided to England 1.3.50
2397	Pte.	SEYMOUR Henry	M	-	Left sick at Ramnuggar 17.2.49
2179	Pte.	SEYMOUR Thomas	M	G	Invalided to England 1.2.51
1970	Pte.	SHERIDAN John	M	G	Invalided to England 1.2.51
1651	Cpl.	SILVER Daniel	M	G	Invalided to England 1.2.51
2458	Pte.	SINCLAIR John (2)	M	G	Died 12.3.49
2023	Pte.	SKELTON Benjamin	M	G	Died 14.6.50
648	Qr.Mst.Sjt.	SLEIGHTER G.	M	G	Dead
1155	Pte.	SLIGHT William	M	-	Left sick at Mooltan
1209	Cpl.	SMART David	M	-	Left wounded at Mooltan, invalided 1.3.50
1752	Pte.	SMITH George	M	-	Left sick at Mooltan, died 21.3.49
2398	Pte.	SMITH Joseph	M	G	Invalided to England 1.3.50
2235	Pte.	SMITH Richard	M	-	Killed in Action 12.9.48
1981	Pte.	SMITH Thomas	M	-	Left sick at Mooltan, died 31.3.49
2576	Pte.	SORDEN	-	G	Died 11.8.51
2165	Pte.	STAGG Henry E.	M	G	Killed in Action 21.2.49
2276	Pte.	STANNAGE John	M	-	Left sick at Mooltan
1790	Cpl.	STANFORD Richard	M	-	Left sick at Mooltan
1543	Pte.	STANDFORD Thomas	M	-	Left sick at Mooltan
2007	Pte.	STAUNTON John	M	G	Invalided to England 1.2.51
	Lt.Col.	STRICKLAND C.L.	-	-	Died 31.7.48
706	Sjt.	SULLIVAN James	M	G	Died 13.7.50
2219	Pte.	SULLIVAN John	M	-	Invalided to England 1.3.50
2234	Pte.	SULLIVAN Michael	M	-	Left sick at Mooltan
2277	Pte.	SULLIVAN Timothy	M	-	Left wounded at Mooltan
2220	Pte.	SULLIVAN William	M	G	Invalided to England 1.3.50
2278	Pte.	SWEETMAN Charles	-	-	Left sick at Ramnuggar 17.2.49

1250	Pte.	TATTERSHALL Henry	M	-	Killed in Action 9.9.48
2461	Pte.	TAYLOR Jervis	M	G	Invalided to England 1.2.51
1976	Pte.	TAYLOR Michael	M	-	Sick to Feroze 16.12.48
1529	Pte.	THORPE William	M	G	Died 3.6.49
2362	Pte.	TIBEANDO Charles	M	G	Died 16.5.49
1075	Sjt.	TIGHE James	M	G	Dead
2222	Pte.	TIGHE James	M	G	Discharge 10.5.50
2053	Pte.	TOOLE Christopher	M	-	Left wounded at Mooltan
2462	Pte.	TOOLE Michael	M	-	Left sick at Ramnuggar, to England 1.3.50
1112	Pte.	TORPEY Denis	M	-	Wounded to Feroze 16.12.48 Discharge 10.5.50

* see below for TRAVERS

1773	Cpl.	VANCE Arthur	M	-	Left sick at Ramnuggar
904	Clr.Sjt.	VINCE John	M	G	Died 12.6.49
2280	Pte.	WALSH Andrew	M	G	Killed in Action 21.2.49
1512	Pte.	WEIR John	M	-	Died of Wounds 10.9.48
1805	Pte.	WELSH John	M	-	Died 6.11.49
1630	Cpl.	WESTRON Henry	M	-	Died of Wounds 17.9.48
1982	Pte.	WHELAN Jeremiah	M	-	Died 3.1.49
1830	Pte.	WHELAN Denis	M	-	Sick to Feroze 16.12.48, Died 17.11.49
1188	Pte.	WHITE William	M	G	Wounded, invalided to England 1.3.50
1237	Pte.	WHITEHEAD Samuel	M	G	Killed in Action 21.2.49
1825	Pte.	WILLIAMSON George	M	G	Invalided to England 1.2.51
1836	Pte.	WILLIAMS William	M	G	Died 19.10.50
1949	Cpl.	WILSON William	M	G	Died 13.11.50
2468	Pte.	WOODS Andrew	M	-	Left sick at Mooltan, to England 1.2.51
1711	Pte.	WOOLSEY Samual	M	G	Invalided to England 1.2.51
1354	Pte.	WRENN James	M	G	Invalided to England 1.2.51
928	Clr.Sjt.	WRIGHT Samuel	M	G	Died 7.1.51
	Lt.Col.	YOUNG G.D.	M	G	Died 20.2.50
*	Ensign	TRAVERS R.H.	M	-	Promoted Lieutenant 24th Foot 14.1.49

The following were at the Depot in Lahore and did not take part in any of the actions:-

2111	Pte.	AHERN John	-	-	Died 6.10.49
2298	Pte.	BULGER Patrick	-	-	Died 8.9.48
1389	.Pte.	MINSHALL William	-	-	Died 3.12.48
864	Pte.	MORGAN James	-	-	Died 25.2.50
2476	Pte.	MURPHY Thomas	-	-	Died 2.8.48
2342	Pte.	NOBLE Charles	-	-	Died 2.11.48
1925	Pte.	RICHARDS Richard	-	-	Died 28.9.48
2457	Pte.	SHEEHY Bryan	-	-	Died 1.12.48
2375	Pte.	SKINNER Robert	-	-	Died 25.3.49
2539	Pte.	SULLIVAN Maurice	-	-	Died 12.2.49
2145	Pte.	WILKIN John	-	-	Died 3.8.48

* * *

SUBORDINATE MEDICAL SERVANTS ATTACHED

	Steward	BAKER C.	M	G	Transferred to Artillery
	Acting Apothecary	WHELAN W.J.	M	G	Transferred to 3rd Dragoons

1147	Sjt.	SHEA John	-	-	Died Lahore 1.9.48
424	Sjt.	O'LONERGAN Michael	-	-	Invalided to England 1.3.50
2163	Pte.	BOOTH James	-	-	Invalided to England 3.6.49
708	Pte.	BROSNAHAN John	-	-	Invalided to England 9.2.49
467	Pte.	CONNORS Miles	-	-	Invalided to England 1.3.50
664	Pte.	DREW John	-	-	Invalided to England 1.2.51
1594	Pte.	GEORGE Richard	-	-	Invalided to England 1.3.50
618	Pte.	GUINAN John	-	-	Invalided to England 1.2.51
1681	Pte.	MAHON William	-	-	Invalided to England 9.2.49
1555	Pte.	BROWN Job	-	-	Invalided to England 9.2.49
2137	Pte.	WALTON Samuel	-	-	Invalided

* * *

24th FOOT

2870	Pte.	AFFLICK Samuel	-	G	Died 17.9.49
2762	Pte.	ALEXANDER John	C	G	Died 27.5.49
2224	Pte.	ALLCOCK Thomas	C	G ·	Died 16.7.50
829	Pte.	ALLEN Henry	C	G	Died 15.9.49
1316	Sjt.	ALLMAN Samuel	-	G	Discharged free in India 1.9.49, Bandmaster 7 N.I.
2094	Pte.	ALLSWORTH William	-	C	Killed at Chilianwala
1464	Pte.	AMOS John	-	C	Killed at Chilianwala
3035	Pte.	ANDERSON James	-	c	Wounded at Chilianwala
2251	Pte.	ANDREWS Stephen	-	C	Killed at Chilianwala
2994	Pte.	ANDREWS William	C	G	Wounded at Chilianwala
1482	Pte.	ANSON Robert	C	-	Died of Wounds received at Chilianwala 21.7.49
Attached	Lieut.	ARCHER J.H. (96th)	C	G	Wounded in Chilianwala, rejoined 96th.
2784	Pte.	ARMITT Joseph	C	-	Killed at Chilianwala
1433	Pte.	ARNOLD Frederick	C	G	Found Dead 2.1.51
2835	Pte.	ASH James	C	G	Wounded at Chilianwala
2206	Pte.	ATCHESON John	C	-	Died 18.7.49
2785	Cpl.	ATKINSON John	C	G	Invalided 15.8.49, to England 10.2.50
2821	Pte.	ATKINSON Thomas	C	-	Killed at Chilianwala
3094	Pte.	ATTWELL Jonah	C	-	Died of wounds received at Chilianwala 18.1.49
2103	Pte.	BAGELY Joseph	C	G	Died 13.11.50
1262	Cpl.	BAILEY George	Medal only		Granted free passage to New South Wales as Military Settler 10.5.50
2865	Pte.	BAILEY Stephen	C	G	Wounded at Chilianwala
1255	Pte.	BAILEY William Henry	C	-	Killed at Chilianwala
	Ensign	BAILLIE W.D.H.	C	G	Lieutenant 14.1.49
2560	Pte.	BAKER John	C	G	Wounded at Chilianwala
1853	Cpl.	BAKER John	C	G	Wounded at Chilianwala
2531	Pte.	BANCROFT Joseph	C	G	Died 15.7.50
2928	Pte.	BARBER James	C	-	Died of Wounds 14.1.49
1451	Pte.	BARKER John	C	G	Free discharge 1.2.51
1330	Pte.	BARLING George	C		Wounded at Chilianwala, died 14.2.50
2715	Pte.	BARLOW John	C	-	Wounded at Chilianwala
2930	Pte.	BARNES Charles	C	-	Killed at Chilianwala
2972	Pte.	BARNETT William	C	-	Killed at Chilianwala

2764	Pte.	BARR Edward	C	-	Killed at Chilianwala
2656	Pte.	BARRETT Joseph	C	-	Wounded at Chilianwala, died 13.8.49
1865	Pte.	BARRINGTON George	C	-	Killed at Chilianwala
2658	Pte.	BARRY John	C	-	Killed at Chilianwala
	Capt.	BAZALGETTE Louis H.	C	G	Wounded at Chilianwala
1648	Pte.	BEAVAN Michael	C	-	Wounded at Chilianwala, discharged by purchase 11.9.49, in England
864	Pte.	BEETLESTONE Francis	C	-	Killed at Chilianwala
1956	Pte.	BETSON Michael	C	-	Killed at Chilianwalla
1161	Pte.	BENNETT Charles	C	G	Free discharge to England 16.2.50
2645	Pte.	BENNETT Henry	C	-	Wounded at Chilianwala, invalided 6.2.49, to England 10.5.49
2872	Pte.	BENTLEY James	C	-	Killed at Chilianwala
2376	Sjt.	BERRINGTON Joseph	C	G	Discharged by purchase to England 23.10.50
	Lieut.	BERRY George F.	C	G	Wounded at Chilianwala, promoted Capttain 20.10.49
937	Pte.	BIBB John	Medal only		Died of wounds received at Sadoolapore
2497	Pte.	BIDDLE Thomas	C	-	Killed at Chilianwala
2102	Pte.	BINGHAM James	C	-	Wounded at Chilianwala
3127	Pte.	BINGHAM Samuel	C	-	Wounded at Chilianwala
2483	Pte.	BIRD George	C	-	Killed at Chilianwala
1402	Sjt.	BIRD Thomas	C	G	Wounded at Chilianwala
1827	Sjt.	BISHOP Edward	C	G	Wounded at Chilianwala
2222	Pte.	BLANCH William	C	G	Died 7.6.49
	Capt.	CLACKFORD A.G.	C	G	Promoted Major 14.1.49
2472	Pte.	BLEWER William	C	-	Wounded at Chilianwala, invalided 4.9.49, to England 7.2.50
1806	Pte.	BOMAN James	C	-	Killed at Chilianwala
2451	Pte.	BONE Samuel	C	G	Wounded at Chilianwala
2696	Pte.	BONE William	C	-	Killed at Chiliawala
2798	Pte.	BOURKE John	C	-	Wounded at Chilianwala
2625	Pte.	BOURNES James	C	-	Wounded at Chilianwala
2394	Pte.	BOYLE Thomas	C	-	Wounded at Chilianwala
1389	Pte.	BOWMAN David	C	-	Wounded at Chilianwala, given free discharge to England 1.2.51
2960	Pte.	BRADBROOK John	C	-	Killed at Chilianwala
1135	Sjt.	BRANAGAN Owen	C	G	Wounded at Chilianwala
1236	Cpl.	BRENNAN John	C	G	Discharge - purchase 2.10.49, in Band, 1 Life Guards London
1523	Pte.	BREWER James	C	-	Killed at Chilianwala
1006	Sjt.	BREWOOD John	C	G	Sent home for free discharge 1.2.51
1830	Sjt.	BRITTAIN Edward	C	G	Died 26.8.50
2921	Pte.	BRITTAIN Frederick	C	-	Discharged by purchase at Agra 1.9.49
2496	Pte.	BRITTAIN George	C	-	Wounded at Chilianwala
2920	Pte.	BRITTON William	C	G	Wounded at Chilianwala
1452	Pte.	BROOKMAN Charles	C	-	Wounded at Chilianwala, invalided 4.9.49, to England 7.2.50
	Lt.Col.	BROOKS Robert	C	-	Commanded 24th at Chilianwala, Killed in Action
2489	Pte.	BROUGHTON Thomas	C	-	Wounded at Chilianwala, invalided 7.9.49 to England 7.2.50
2487	Pte.	BROWN James	C	G	Wounded at Chilianwala

	No.	Rank	Name			Remarks
	2925	Pte.	BROWN John	C	G	Wounded at Chilianwala
		Capt.	BROWN William G.	C	G	Wounded at Chilianwala, promoted Major 1!
	2926	Pte.	BRUCE John	C	-	Wounded at Chilianwala
	1458	Cpl.	BUDGEN William	C	-	Died of wounds 14.1.49
	1301	Pte.	BURCHETT Richard	C	-	Killed at Chilianwala
	2322	Pte.	BURGESS John	C	-	Killed at Chillianwala
	3093	Pte.	BURKE Martin	C	G	Wounded at Chilianwala
See Page 33 for * Burton John	2698	Pte.	BURTON James	C	-	Killed at Chilianwala
	1608	Pte.	BUTCHER James	C	-	Killed at Chilianwala
	844	Pte.	BYERS Joseph	C	-	Killed at Chilianwala
	1831	Pte.	BYRNE Terence	C	G	Died 30.5.49
	1125	Pte.	BYRNE Thomas	C	-	Killed at Chilianwala
	3128	Pte.	CALE James	C	G	Died 26.5.50
	1401	Pte.	CAMDEN Charles	C	G	Wounded at Chilianwala, died 15.12.49
	2615	Pte.	CAMPBELL Robert	C	-	Killed at Chilianwala
	2418	Pte.	CARPENTER Thomas	C	-	Killed at Chilianwala
	3038	Pte.	CARRIER John	C	-	Killed at Chilianwala
	1812	Pte.	CARTER John	C	-	Died of wounds received at Chilianwala 3(
	2294	Pte.	CARTER Samuel	C	-	Killed at Chilianwala
	2642	Pte.	CAREY John	C	-	Wounded at Chilianwala
	2486	Pte.	CAVANAGH Francis	C	G	Transferred to 61st Foot 1.10.49
	2041	Pte.	CAVILL Charles	C	G	Wounded at Chilianwala, died 29.12.50
	2984	Pte.	CHANNING James G.	C	-	Wounded at Chilianwala, invalided 4.9.49 to England 7.2.50
	3182	Pte.	CHAPPEL Thomas	C	-	Killed at Chilianwala
	2362	Cpl.	CHARTERS William	C	-	Wounded at Chilianwala
	2326	Pte.	CHEESE Joseph	C	-	Wounded at Chilianwala, invalided 6.2.49 to England 10.5.49
	1761	Pte.	CHITTLE Thomas	C	G	Died 2.11.49
	3032	Pte.	CLARK James	C	-	Killed at Chilianwala
	3161	Pte.	CLARK George	C	G	Discharged by purchase, to England 16.10
	2541	Pte.	CLARKE Edward	C	-	Wounded at Chilianwala, invalided 4.9.49 to England 7.2.50
	1414	Cpl.	CLARKE James	C	G	Died 26.11.50
		Lieut.	CLEVELAND D.D. (98th)	Medal only		Joined 14.3.49 (24th), rejoined 98th
	1425	Pte.	CLIFFORD Daniel	C	-	Killed at Chilianwala
	2367	Pte.	CLUNEN Thomas	C	-	Killed at Chilianwala
	1931	Pte.	COATES Richard John	C	-	Killed at Chilianwala
	2491	Pte.	COCKERTON Robert	C	-	Killed at Chilianwala
	1180	Sjt.Maj.	COFFEE John	C	-	Killed at Chilianwala
	1321	Pte.	COLLETT Thomas	C	G	Wounded at Chilianwala
	1754	Clr.Sjt.	COLLINS James	Medal only		Killed in Action Sadolapore 3.12.48
	3087	Pte.	COLLINS John	C	-	Wounded at Chilianwala
	2604	Pte.	COLLINS Thomas	C	-	Wounded at Chilianwala
		Ensign.	COLLIS Hector C.B.	C	-	Killed at Chilianwala
	3098	Pte.	CONNELLY Michael	C	-	Wounded at Chilianwala, invalided 4.9.49 to England 7.2.50
	2707	Pte.	CONNOLLY James	C	-	Killed at Chilianwala

3030	Pte.	CONNOLLY Martin	C	G	Wounded at Chilianwala
2874	Pte.	COOK Daniel	C	-	Wounded at Chilianwala, died 10.12.50
1938	Pte.	COOK John	C	G	Wounded at Chilianwala, died 2.10.50
2236	Pte.	CORK Henry	C	-	Killed at Chilianwala
1833	Pte.	COULT William	C	-	Killed at Chilianwala
2750	Pte.	CRAVEN Joseph	C	G	Wounded at Chilianwala
2453	Pte.	CRESSWELL Thomas	C	-	Killed at Chilianwala
1232	Pte.	CRICK George	C	G	Wounded at Chilianwala
	Lieut.	CROKER Richard H.	C	G	Wounded at Chilianwala, promoted Captain 15. 1.49
2516	Pte.	CROSS William	C	-	Wounded at Chilianwala
2751	Pte.	CROSS William	C	-	Killed at Chilianwala
3057	Pte.	CROW Charles	C	G	Wounded at Chilianwala
2650	Pte.	CROWDY John	C	G	Wounded at Chilianwala
2831	Pte.	CUMMINGS John	C	G	Wounded at Chilianwala
2875	Pte.	CUTHBIRTH William	C	-	Killed at Chilianwala
3102	Pte.	DALY Patrick	C	-	Killed at Chilianwala
2162	Pte.	DAVIES Richard	C	G	Died 24.11.49
2841	Pte.	DAVIS James	C	G	Wounded at Chilianwala
3090	Pte.	DAVIS George	C	G	Wounded at Chilianwala
3009	Pte.	DAVIS William	C	-	Died of wounds received at Chilianwala 27.1.49
1854	Clr.Sjt.	DAVIS William	C	-	Killed at Chilianwala
2136	Sjt.	DAY Fergus	C	G	Wounded at Chilianwala
3050	Pte.	DAWSON Richard	C	G	Wounded at Chilianwala
2692	Pte.	DEAN George	C	-	Killed at Chilianwala
2533	Pte.	DEANS John	C	-	Wounded at Chilianwala
1140	Pte.	DEASY Thomas	C	G	Wounded at Chilianwala
1243	Pte.	DELLER James	C	G	Wounded at Chilianwala, grabted free discharge in England 1.2.51
3126	Pte.	DELMAGE James	C	-	Killed at Chilianwala
3059	Pte.	DEVANEY Patrick	C	-	Killed at Chilianwala
804	Drummer	DEVINE John	C	G	Died 17.7.50
1254	Pte.	DIX Frederick	C	G	Wounded at Chilianwala, died 18.9.49
2876	Pte.	DIXON Henry	C	G	Wounded at Chilianwala
1765	Pte.	DOLLERY George	C	G	Wounded at Chilianwala
2315	Sjt.	DONOGHUE Timothy	C	G	Discharged by purchase to Europe 2.10.49
2242	Drummer	DOUGHTY Edward	C	-	Killed at Chilianwala
3029	Pte.	DOWSETT James	C	G	Wounded at Chilianwala
2589	Pte.	DOYLE Patrick	C	-	Wounded at Chilianwala
3164	Pte.	DRISCALL Michael	C	G	Wounded at Chilianwala
1742	Pte.	DUDLEY James	C	-	Killed at Chilianwala
2050	Pte.	DUFFAN Wm.Jansen,Sanders	C	-	Killed at Chilianwala
2638	Pte.	DYER John	C	G	Wounded at Chilianwala, died 4.10.50
2079	Cpl.	EAMES George	C	-	Killed at Chilianwala
1120	Clr.Sjt.	EASTALL Frederick	C	G	Promoted Sjt. Major 14.1.49
2792	Pte.	EBBARY John	C.	G	Wounded at Chilianwala, invalided 15.8.49 to England 16.2.50
2189	Pte.	EDWARDS James	C	-	Killed at Chilianwala

2421	Pte.	EDWARDS John	Medal only		Died 26.1.49
2755	Pte.	EDMUNDS Robert	C	-	Killed at Chilianwala
3060	Pte.	EGAN Garrett	C	-	Killed at Chilianwala
3010	Pte.	EGELTON Charles	C	G	Wounded at Chilianwala
801	Pte.	EGGINTON Joseph	C	-	Killed at Chilianwala
1477	Pte.	EHEMELY William	C	-	Killed at Chilianwala
1101	Pte.	ELDERSHALL Thomas	C	-	Wounded at Chilianwala, invalided and died 28.3.49
3003	Pte.	ELLIOTT Edward	C	-	Wounded at Chilianwala, invalided 4.9.49, to England 7.2.50
3004	Pte.	ELLIOTT James	C	-	Killed at Chilianwala
1656	Pte.	ELLIOTT John	C	G	Wounded at Chilianwala
2842	Pte.	ELLIS Thomas	C	-	Killed at Chilianwala
3068	Pte.	ENGLISH Samuel	C	-	Killed at Chilianwala
2657	Pte.	ENRIGHT John	C	-	Killed at Chilianwala
2662	Pte.	EVANS George	C	-	Killed at Chilianwala
2983	Pte.	EVANS George	C	G	Wounded at Chilianwala
2161	Pte.	EVANS Thomas	C	-	Wounded at Chilianwala, invalided 4.9.49 to England 16.2.50
1609	Pte.	EVEREST Edward	C	-	Killed at Chilianwala
3104	Pte.	FAHY Michael	C	-	Wounded at Chilianwala, invalided 4.9.49, to England 7.2.50
2946	Pte.	FARMER Henry	C	-	Killed at Chilianwala
3048	Pte.	FAULKNER George	C	-	Wounded at Chilianwala
2599	Pte.	FERGUSON John	C	-	Killed at Chilianwala
2250	Sjt.	FIELDING George	C	-	Wounded at Chilianwal, invalided 6.2.49, to England 10.5.49
2987	Pte.	FIRTH Abel	Medal only		Died 28.2.49
2768	Pte.	FITZGERALD James	C	-	Wounded at Chilianwala, invalided 28.8.50, to England 1.2.51
1461	Pte.	FLETCHER William	C	-	Killed at Chilianwala
2337	Pte.	FLICKER William	C	G	Sent to England 16.10.50 for discharge by purchase.
2522	Pte.	FLINN James	C	-	Killed at Chilianwala
2664	Pte.	FLYNN Patrick	C	-	Killed at Chilianwala
1950	Sjt.	FOLEY Michael	C	G	Deputy Provost Marshal 3rd Inf. Division
2552	Pte.	FOWKE Philip	C	-	Killed at Chilianwala
2490	Pte.	FRANCIS William	C	-	Killed at Chilianwala
3005	Pte.	FRANCIS William	C	G	Wounded at Chilianwala
3070	Pte.	FRENCH John	C	G	Wounded at Chilianwala
	Lieut.	FRERE A.E.	Medal only		Died 9.11.48
2940	Pte.	FRY Edward	C	-	Killed at Chilianwala
Assit. Surgeon		FURLONGE W.J.	C	G	Died 12.12.49
2568	Pte.	GADNEY Richard	C	-	Wounded at Chilianwala, invalided 4.9.49, to England 7.2.50
953	Pte.	GARDNER Thomas	Medal only		Died 18.11.48
1292	Pte.	GARDNER William	C	-	Killed at Chilianwala
1360	Pte.	GARNER William	C	-	Wounded at Chilianwala, granted free discharge 1.2.51
3061	Pte.	GARVIN William	C	G	Died 31.8.49

2305	Pte.	GEORGE George	C	-	Killed at Chilianwala
2518	Pte.	GIBSON George	C	-	Killed at Chilianwala
2569	Pte.	GILES William	C	-	Killed at Chilianwala
2600	Pte.	GILLERAN Michael	C	G	Wounded at Chilianwala
2811	Pte.	GLEESON Martin	C	G	Wounded at Chilianwala
2879	Pte.	GLYNN Dennis	C	G	Wounded at Chilianwala
1539	Pte.	GOLDSWORTHY William	C	G	Wounded at Chilianwala
2565	Pte.	GOLLAND George	C	-	Wounded at Chilianwala, invalided 28.8.50, to England 1.2.51
2944	Pte.	GOODACRE Charles	C	G	Wounded at Chilianwala
1427	Pte.	GOODCHILD James	C	-	Killed at Chilianwala
2058	Pte.	GOODING John	C	-	Wounded at Chilianwala, died 16.1.50
	Lieut.	GOODFELLOW J.C.	M	G	With 10th Foot at Mooltan. 24th Foot 17.2.49
	Surgeon	GORDON Archibald MD	C	G	Rejoined 95th Foot.
	Lieut.	GRAHAM Oliver T.	Medal only		Resigned - Sale of commission 3.4.49
2976	Pte.	GRANDY Thomas	C	-	Killed at Chilianwala
	Lieut.	GRANT Sweton	C	G	Capt. 14.1.49, died 19.10.49
2375	Pte.	GRAY James	C	-	Killed at Chiliawala
3054	Pte.	GREAVES William	C	-	Wounded at Chilianwala, invalided 28.8.50, to England 1.2.51
3067	Pte.	GREEN Charles	C	-	Killed at Chilianwala
3001	Pte.	GREEN Isiah	C	-	Wounded at Chilianwala, invalided 28.8.50, to England 1.2.51
2628	Pte.	GREEN George	C	-	Wounded at Chilianwala
2844	Pte.	GREEN Michael	C	-	Killed at Chilianwala
2494	Pte.	GRIFFIN John	C	-	Wounded at Chilianwala
2880	Pte.	HAFNER William	C	G	Transported for 7 years by General Court Marshal on 5.12.50
3160	Pte.	HAGGAR George	C	G	Discharged by purchase 8.6.50, joined 1 Coy. 1 Bn. H.E.I.6's Arty.
	Lieut.	HALAHAN Robert	-	G	Joined from 18th Foot on the field 21.2.49
2339	Sjt.	HALE John	C	G	Discharged by purchase to England 28.12.50
3120	Pte.	HALFORD Charles	C	-	Wounded at Chilianwala
2929	Pte.	HALL Thomas Smith	C	-	Killed at Chilianwala
1948	Pte.	HANLON James	C	-	Killed at Chilianwala
1546	Pte.	HANSCOMBE Thomas	C	-	Killed at Chilianwala
3013	Pte.	HARDING Richard	C	-	Killed at Chilianwala
2426	Pte.	HARDMAN George	C	-	Killed at Chilianwala
2459	Pte.	HARFIELD John	C	G	Wounded at Chilianwala
2121	Pte.	HARRIS George	C	-	Killed at Chilianwala
	Major	HARRIS Henry William	C	-	Killed at Chilianwala
	Capt.	HARRIS Charles R.	C	-	Brigade Major 5th Bde. Killed at Chilianwala
1655	Cpl.	HARRISON George	C	G	Free dishcrage 1.2.51
2463	Pte.	HARRISON George	C	-	Killed at Chilianwala
	Lt. & Adj.	HARTSHORN W.	C	G	Wounded at Chilianwala
2939	Pte.	HARVEY Benjamin	C	-	Wounded at Chilianwala
2432	Pte.	HASLOCK Robert	C	G	Wounded at Chilianwala
1962	Pte.	HASTON James	C	-	Killed at Chilianwala
2634	Pte.	HATLOW James	C	G	Wounded at Chilianwala

1936	Pte.	HAWKINS Joseph	C	-	Died of wounds received at Chilianwala 15.1.49
1747	Pte.	HAZELL Henry	C	-	Wounded at Chilianwala, invalided 4.9.49, to England 7.2.50
1744	Pte.	HAZELL Richard	C	-	Wounded at Chilianwala
967	Pte.	HEBSON William	C	-	Killed at Chilianwala
2590	Pte.	HENRY Bartholomew	C	-	Killed at Chilianwala
2327	Pte.	HENSHAW John	C	-	Killed at Chilianwala
2635	Pte.	HEPBURN Magnus	C	-	Wounded at Chilianwala
1796	Pte.	HERBERT William	C	G	Discharged by purchase to England 16.10.50
2763	Pte.	HICKES John	C	G	Wounded at Chilianwala
2117	Pte.	HICKS James	C	-	Killed at Chilianwala
2633	Pte.	HICKEY Stephen	C	-	Invalided 15.8.49 to England 16.2.50
1456	Pte.	HILDITCH Samuel	C	G	Wounded at Chilianwala
2828	Pte.	HILL John	C	-	Killed at Chilianwala
2410	Pte.	HILL William	C	G	Wounded at Chilianwala
1270	Pte.	HILLMAN John	C	-	Wounded at Chilianwala
2424	Pte.	HILSDEN George	C	-	Wounded at Chilianwala, died 15.3.50
	Ensign	HINDE Henry John	C	G	Lieut. 14.1.49
1990	Sjt.	HIZZARD Robert	C	G	Dead
2406	Pte.	HODGEN Adam	C	-	Wounded at Chilianwala
2985	Pte.	HOLLEY Joseph	C	-	Wounded at Chilianwala, invalided 6.2.49, to England 10.5.49
2546	Pte.	HOLME Robert	C	-	Wounded at Chilianwala
2586	Pte.	HONEY William	C	-	Wounded at Chilianwala
1752	Pte.	HOPKINS James	C	-	Wounded at Chilianwala, invalided 6.2.49, to England 10.5.49
2423	Pte.	HOPKINS William	C	-	Killed at Chilianwala
1939	Pte.	HORSFALL John	C	-	Killed at Chilianwala
2019	Cpl.	HORSLEY Robert	C	-	Wounded at Chilianwala, invalided 4.9.49, returned England 7.2.50
2386	Pte.	HOULTON William	C	G	Wounded at Chilianwala
2684	Pte.	HOULSTON Daniel	C	-	Killed at Chilianwala
1960	Pte.	HOUSE John	C	G	Died 13.8.50
1079	Cpl.	HOWELL Francis	C	-	Killed at Chilianwala
2263	Pte.	HOWSE Charles	C	G	Wounded at Chilianwala
2974	Pte.	HUCKER William	C	-	Killed at Chilianwala
2992	Pte.	HUDGELL Henry	C	G	Wounded at Chilianwala
2772	Pte.	HUGHES Solomon	C	G	Wounded at Chilianwala
1781	Pte.	HUGHES Thomas	C	G	Wounded at Chilianwala
3028	Pte.	HUMPHREYS Thomas	-	G	Died 29.5.49
2703	Pte.	HUNT James	Medal only		Died 8.12.48
2572	Pte.	HUNTER John	C	-	Killed at Chilianwala
3105	Pte.	HURLEY Michael	C	G	Wounded at Chilianwala
2914	Pte.	HUTLEY William	Medal only		Died 21.12.48
2624	Pte.	HUTTON George	C	-	Died of wounds received at Chilianwala 3.2.49
2743	Pte.	INDLE Edward	C	-	Killed at Chilianwala
2324	Pte.	INTON John Edward	C	-	Killed at Chilianwala
2613	Pte.	IRELAND William	C	G	Wounded at Chilianwala

2412	Pte.	JAMES Alfred	C	G	Wounded at Chilianwala
2744	Pte.	JARVIS John	C	-	Wounded at Chilianwala
1430	Pte.	JERVIS William	C	-	Killed at Chilianwala
1977	Pte.	JOBLIN Thomas	C	-	Killed at Chilianwala
1677	Pte.	JOHNSON Benjamin	C	-	Killed at Chilianwala
1763	Pte.	JOHNSON Edward	C	-	Killed at Chilianwala
2558	Pte.	JOHNSON John	C	G	Wounded at Chilianwala
2819	Pte.	JOHNSON William	C	G	Wounded at Chilianwala
2266	Pte.	JONES John	C	-	Wounded at Chilianwala
2803	Pte.	JONES Thomas	C	-	Wounded at Chilianwala, invalided 6.2.49, to England 10.5.49
2977	Pte.	JOWERS William	C	-	Wounded at Chilianwala, invalided 28.8.50, to England 1.2.51
2653	Pte.	KAVANAGH Richard	C	-	Wounded at Chilianwala
2577	Pte.	KEABLE Richard	C	G	Wounded at Chilianwala
2774	Pte.	KEEGAN Patrick	C	-	Wounded at Chilianwala, invalided 6.2.49, to England 10.5.49
2452	Pte.	KEEN Thomas	C	G	Wounded at Chilianwala
2467	Pte.	KEFFORD Thomas	C	-	Wounded at Chilianwala
3055	Pte.	KELLY James	C	-	Killed at Chilianwala
2883	Pte.	KELLY John	C	G	Insane, invalided 11.2.50, sent to England 12.3.51
2810	Pte.	KELLY Mathew	C	-	Wounded at Chilianwala
1573	Pte.	KING James	C	-	Killed at Chilianwala
2919	Pte.	KELLY Patrick	C	G	Wounded at Chilianwala
2955	Pte.	KELSON Thomas	C	-	Killed at Chilianwala
2947	Pte.	KEMP Charles	C	G	Wounded at Chilianwala
1943	Pte.	KENNEDY Patrick	C	-	Wounded at Chilianwala
2126	Pte.	KENTISH William	C	-	Wounded at Chilianwala
2457	Pte.	KIDGER George	C	G	Wounded at Chilianwala
1799	Pte.	KILLEEN James	C	-	Killed at Chilianwala
2951	Pte.	KILPATRICK William	C	G	Wounded at Chilianwala
2958	Pte.	KING James	C	-	Wounded at Chilianwala
1210	Pte.	KINNING John	C	-	Killed at Chilianwala
2652	Pte.	KNIGHT Joseph	C	-	Wounded at Chilianwala
3014	Pte.	LAING Robert	C	-	Killed at Chilianwala
1197	Pte.	LAKE John	C	-	Killed at Chilianwala
1228	Pte.	LAKIN William	C	-	Killed at Chilianwala
2416	Pte.	LAMB John	C	-	Killed at Chilianwala
3097	Pte.	LAMBERT Ebenezer	C	G	Wounded at Chilianwala
2676	Pte.	LANCASTER Charles	C	-	Killed at Chilianwala
2797	Pte.	LANCASTER Robert	Medal only		Invalided 4.9.49, to England 7.2.50
2849	Pte.	LANCASTER Thomas	C	-	Killed at Chilianwala
2464	Pte.	LANDER Charles	C	-	Killed at Chilianwala
2858	Pte.	LANG Francis	C	-	Killed at Chilianwala
1420	Pte.	LAWRENCE Charles	C	-	Killed at Chilianwala
2438	Pte.	LEA James	C	G	Died 11.5.50
1447	Sjt.	LEAR Thomas	C	-	Killed at Chilianwala

3155	Pte.	LEARY Cornelius	C	-	Wounded at Chilianwala, invalided 6.2.49, to England 10.5.49
	Capt.	LEE Charles	C	-	Killed at Chilianwala
2968	Pte.	LEES Cartwright	C	G	Wounded at Chilianwala
2429	Pte.	LETFORD Charles	C	G	Wounded at Chilianwala
2108	Sjt.	LETFORD Henry	C	-	Wounded at Chilianwala
1723	Pte.	LINFORD Henry	C	G	Wounded at Sadoolapore 3.12.48
2219	Pte.	LISCOCKS Samuel	C	G	Wounded at Chilianwala, died 12.9.50
1974	Pte.	LIST Thomas	C	-	Killed at Chilianwala
2756	Pte.	LLOYD Oliver	C	-	Killed at Chilianwala
1835	Cpl.	LOADSMAN Benjamin William	C	-	Wounded at Chilianwala
2515	Pte.	LOCK James William	C	-	Wounded at Chilianwala, invalided 15.8.49, to England 16.2.50
2997	Pte.	LOMAS Thomas	C	-	Died of wounds received at Chilianwala 27.1.49
2961	Pte.	LONG George	C	-	Wounded at Chilianwala, invalided 4.9.49, to England 7.2.50
1261	Pte.	LONG William Henry	C	G	Wounded at Chilianwala
	Lieut.	LUTMAN John Henry	C	G	Capt. 14.1.49
2890	Pte.	LYNCH Thomas	Medal only		Died 8.12.48
	Lieut.	MACPHERSON Andrew J.	C	-	Wounded at Chilianwala, Capt. 14.1.49
2734	Pte.	McCORMICK James	C	-	Wounded at Chilianwala, invalided 28.8.50, to England 1.2.51
2729	Pte.	McCROHAN Dennis	C	G	Wounded at Chiliaawala
3018	Pte.	McCULLOCH John	C	-	Killed at Chilianwala
2385	Pte.	McDANIEL David	C	G	Wounded at Chilianwala
2504	Pte.	MAGILL Benjamin	C	-	Killed at Chilianwala
2508	Pte.	McGRATH Patrick	C	-	Wounded at Chilianwala, invalided 6.2.49, to England 10.5.49
3075	Pte.	McCORMICK Michael	C	-	Dead
2893	Pte.	McGREGOR Alexander	C	G	Died 17.9.49
2851	Pte.	McMULLEN Joseph	C	-	Killed at Chilianwala
2971	Pte.	McRARY John	C	-	Killed at Chilianwala
2894	Pte.	MACKEY Thomas	C	-	Killed at Chilianwala
2174	Pte.	MACOLEY Peter	C	-	Killed at Chilianwala
2663	Q.M.Sjt.	MADDEN Thomas	C	G	Promoted Quartermaster 12.10.49
2234	Pte.	MADGE John	C	G	Wounded at Chilianwala
2892	Pte.	MAGINNIS Alexander	C	G	Wounded at Chilianwala
3042	Pte.	MANGAN Patrick	C	-	Killed at Chilianwala
1303	Pte.	MARCHANT Thomas	C	-	Killed at Chilianwala
2051	Sjt.	MASTERS John	C	G	Died 11.1.50
2943	Pte.	MATHEWS Charles	C	-	Wounded at Chilianwala, invalided 6.2.49, to England 10.5.49
2935	Pte.	MATHEWS William	C	G	Wounded at Chilianwala
2267	Pte.	MAYO Charles	C	-	Killed at Chilianwala
973	Pte.	MAYO Thomas	C	G	Wounded at Chilianwala, invalided 28.8.50, to England 1.2.51
3002	Pte.	MAYS William	C	G	Wounded at Chilianwala
1336	Pte.	MEAD Joseph	C	G	Wounded at Chilianwala
3092	Pte.	MEADE Edwin	C	-	Killed at Chilianwala

2694	Pte.	MEADOWS Joesph	C	G	Wounded at Chilianwala, given free discharge 2.10.49. Joined 1Coy. 1 Batt. Arty.
2610	Pte.	MEDLAM William Henry	C	-	Killed at Chilianwala
1174	Pte.	MEEDS Henry	C	-	Killed at Chilianwala
3074	Pte.	MEEK James	C	-	Wounded at Chilianwala, invalided 4.9.49, to England 7.2.50
2777	Pte.	MEVILLE William	Medal only		Died 8.12.48
2398	Pte.	MERITON Henry	C	-	Wounded at Chilianwala
2208	Pte.	MIDDLETON William	C	G	Wounded at Chilianwala, died 26.10.49
2918	Pte.	MILLER Robert	C	G	Wounded at Chilianwala
2626	Pte.	MILLS Samuel	C	G	Dishcarged by purchase 19.1.50 to England
2732	Pte.	MITCHELL Charles	C	-	Killed at Chilianwala
3143	Pte.	MOHAN John	C	-	Killed at Chilianwala
1968	Pte.	MOORE Michael	C	-	Killed at Chilianwala
2739	Pte.	MOORE William	C	-	Wounded at Chilianwala, invalided 28.8.50, to England 1.2.51
2754	Pte.	MORRIS Evans	C	-	Killed at Chilianwala
1748	Pte.	MORRIS James	C	-	Died of wounds received at Chilianwala 16.1.49
2779	Pte.	MORRIS Robert	C	G	Died 24.5.49
2085	Pte.	MORRISH Thomas	C	-	Killed at Chilianwala
2220	Pte.	MORTON Joseph	C	-	Killed at Chilianwala
818	Pte.	MURPHY Alexander	C	-	Wounded at Chilianwala, invalided 6.2.49, to England 16.2.50
2640	Pte.	MURPHY John	C	-	Wounded at Chilianwala, invalided 4.9.49 to England 7.2.50
2646	Pte.	MURPHY John	C	-	Killed at Chilianwala
2666	Pte.	MURPHY Philip	C	-	Killed at Chilianwala
2596	Pte.	MURPHY Tede	C	-	Killed at Chilianwala
2681	Pte.	MURPHY Thomas	C	G	Wounded at Chilianwala
2898	Pte.	MURRAY John	C	-	Wounded at Chilianwala
2614	Pte.	MURPHY Morgan	C	-	Wounded at Chilianwala, died 20.6.50
2231	Pte.	MURTHA James	Medal only		Killed at Sadoolapore 3.12.48
673	Cpl.	NEALE Benjamin	C	G	Invalided 5.9.50 to England 1.2.51
2444	Pte.	NEALE Henry	C	G	Wounded at Chilianwala, died 29.5.50
3011	Pte.	NEVARD William	C	-	Killed at Chilianwala
2867	Pte.	NEWALL George	C	-	Wounded at Chilianwala, invalided 28.8.50, to England 1.2.51
1436	Pte.	NIMMO Thomas	C	G	Died 22.3.50
2728	Pte.	NISBETT Andrew	C	-	Wounded at Chilianwala
2900	Pte.	NICHOLS John	C	G	Died 28.6.50
2995	Pte.	NICHOLLS William	C	-	Killed at Chilianwala
2606	Pte.	NEWMAN Joseph	C	-	Killed at Chilianwala
2802	Pte.	NOWLAN William	C	G	Wounded at Chilianwala
3156	Pte.	OAKLEY William	C	-	Killed at Chilianwala
2473	Pte.	O'BRIEN Charles	C	G	Wounded at Chilianwala
596	Armoured Sjt.	O'BRIEN W.	C	G	Died 27.4.50
2008	Cpl.	O'BRIEN Patrick	C	G	Wounded at Chilianwala
2505	Pte.	O'CONNOR James	C	-	Killed at Chilianwala
2672	Pte.	O'DONOGHUE John Timothy	C	-	Killed at Chilianwala

3134	Pte.	O'NEIL James	C	-	Wounded at Chilianwala, invalided 15.8.49, to England 16.2.50
2901	Pte.	O'NEIL John	C	-	Wounded at Chilianwala
2924	Pte.	ORROCK Hugh	C	G	Wounded at Chilianwala
1850	C.Sjt.	ORTON Henry	C	-	Wounded at Chilianwala
2988	Pte.	OSBOURNE Thomas	C	-	Killed at Chilianwala
2057	Pte.	OVERTON John M.	C	-	Killed at Chilianwala
1746	Pte.	PACE Thomas	C	G	Discharged by purchase to England 6.12.49
1293	Pte.	PARKER Thomas	C	-	Killed at Chilianwala
1549	Cpl.	PARKMAN Charles	C	G	Free discharge 1.2.51
2595	Pte.	PARRY Hugh	C	G	Transferred to 29th Foot 28.2.50
1809	C.Sjt.	PARTRIDGE Thomas G.	C	G	Wounded at Chilianwala
1701	Pte.	PATIENCE James	C	-	Killed at Chilianwala
1757	Cpl.	PATIENCE William	Medal only		
2217	Cpl.	PATTENDEN William	C	-	Killed at Chilianwala
2131	Pte.	PAYNE John	C	G	Wounded at Chilianwala
	Lieut.	PAYNE O.B.	C	-	Killed at Chilianwala
	Major	PAYNTER Howell	C	-	Wounded at Chilianwala, Promoted Lt.Col. Commanding 24th 14.1.49
2563	Pte.	PEARCE George	C	G	Wounded at Chilianwala
814	Pte.	PEARSON William	C	-	Killed at Chilianwala
2796	Pte.	PEEL Abraham	C	G	Wounded at Chilianwala
2377	Pte.	PENNINGTON Charles	C	G	Wounded at Chilianwala
	Ensign.	PENNYCUICK Alexander	C	-	Killed at Chilianwala
	Lt.Col.	PENNYCUIK John CB KH	C	-	Commanded 5th Bde. at Chilianwala. Killed 13.1.49
2644	Pte.	PERRY Henry	C	G	Dead
2950	Pte.	PESTELL George	C	G	Wounded at Chilianwala, transferred to 32nd Foot 1.11.48
1191	Pte.	PETTIT Moses	C	G	Granted free discharge 1.2.51
2003	Pte.	PHEALAN Michale	C	-	Killed at Chilianwala
1564	Pte.	PHILLIPS James	C	-	Killed at Chilianwala
2559	Pte.	PHILLIPS John	C	G	Wounded at Chilianwala. Dead.
	Lieut.	PHILLIPS George	C	-	Killed at Chilianwala
1372	Pte.	PHILLIPS Thomas	C	G	Wounded at Chilianwala
1416	Pte.	PHILLIPS Thomas	C	-	Wounded at Chilianwala
	Lieut.	PHILLIPS William	C	-	Killed at Chilianwala
2716	Cpl.	PHIPPS Edward	C	-	Wounded at Chilianwala
3150	Pte.	PIERCE Nicholas	-	G	Died 31.5.49
2868	Pte.	PIKE John	Medal only		Died 17.2.49
	Surgeon.	PITCAIRN G.K.	Medal only		
2678	Pte.	PITTMAN James	C	-	Killed at Chilianwala
1172	C.Sjt.	PLATTS James	C	-	Wounded at Chilianwala, invalided 6.2.49, to England 10.5.49
1434	Pte.	PLAW James	C	G	Granted free discharge 1.2.51
2468	Pte.	PLUMB Henry	C	G	Wounded 3.12.48
2989	Pte.	POPCOCK Thomas	C	-	Killed at Chilianwala
2532	Pte.	POLETON George	C	-	Wounded at Chilianwala
3136	Pte.	POOLE William	C	G	Wounded at Chilianwala

2158	Pte.	PORTER Robert	C	-	Killed at Chilianwala
2368	Pte.	POTTER William	C	-	Wounded at Chilianwala
2392	Cpl.	PRATT David	C	G	Wounded at Chilianwala
1858	Pte.	PRATT John	C	-	Killed at Chilianwala
2854	Pte.	PRATT John	C	G	Dead
2941	Pte.	PRATT Robert	C	-	Killed at Chilianwala
2969	Pte.	PRETTY John	C	G	Wounded at Chilianwala
	Qrt.Mas.	PRICE James	C	G	Died 4.7.49
2164	Pte.	PRIEST Thomas	C	-	Killed at Chilianwala
843	Pte.	PRITCHARD James	C	G	Wounded at Chilianwala
2386	Pte.	PUDDICOMB Joseph	C	G	Wounded at Chilianwala
2334	Pte.	PULLING Nathaniel	C	-	Killed at Chilianwala
2556	Pte.	QUARTERMAINE Samuel	C	G	Died 2.12.50
3140	Pte.	QUIRKE Patrick	C	-	Killed at Chilianwala
2585	Pte.	RAMPLING William	C	-	Killed at Chilianwala
2567	Pte.	READING Henry	C	-	Wounded at Chilianwala
2730	Drummer	REDDING James	C	G	Died 9.8.49
3149	Pte.	REGAN John	C	-	Wounded at Chilianwal, invalided 28.8.50, to England 1.2.51
3148	Pte.	REGAN Thomas	C	-	Killed at Chilianwala
2927	Pte.	REMINGTON William	C	-	Wounded at Chilianwala
3152	Pte.	REYNOLDS Michael	C	-	Wounded at Chilianwala, invalided 28.8.50, to England 1.2.51
2188	Pte.	RICE Charles	Medal only		Died 2.9.49
2307	Pte.	RICHARDS William	C	-	Wounded at Chilianwala, invalided 6.2.49, to England 18.5.49
2780	Pte.	RIDDLE James	C	-	Killed at Chilianwala
2265	Pte.	RIDER William	C	-	Killed at Chilianwala
2855	Pte.	RING James	C	-	Wounded at Chilianwala, invalided 4.9.49, to England 7.2.50
2612	Pte.	RIORDAN Patrick	C	G	Wounded at Chilianwala
2403	Pte.	RIPPIN Joseph	C	-	Wounded at Chilianwala, invalided 28.8.50, to England 1.2.51
2540	Pte.	RIX George	C	G	Wounded at Chilianwala
2905	Pte.	ROBARTS Richard	C	-	Wounded at Chilianwala
1766	Pte.	ROBINSON George	C	G	Wounded at Chilianwala
2165	Pte.	ROBINSON Thomas	C	-	Killed at Chilianwala
2789	Pte.	RICHFORD Christopher	C	-	Killed at Chilianwala
1189	Pte.	ROSTER Thomas	C	-	Killed at Chilianwala
1815	Pte.	ROXBURY Joseph	C	-	Killed at Chilianwala
2209	Pte.	RUNCHEY William	C	-	Killed at Chilianwala
2147	Pte.	RYAN Edward	C	-	Wounded at Chilianwala, invalided 4.9.49, to England 7.2.50
1574	Pte.	SANDERS William	C	G	Granted free discharge 1.2.51
1362	Pte.	SANDERSON Joseph	C	G	Granted free discharge 1.2.51
2292	Pte.	SANDFORD Richard	C	-	Killed at Chilianwala
2458	Pte.	SAUNDERS George	C	-	Killed at Chilianwala
2745	Pte.	SAUNDERS James L.	C	-	Killed at Chilianwala
1203	Pte.	SAVAGE Thomas	C	-	Killed at Chilianwala

2297	Cpl.	SAVAGE William	C	G	Wounded at Chilianwala
3145	Pte.	SCOTT Francis	C	G	Died 28.9.50
1440	Sjt.	SCOTT William	C	G	Wounded at Chilianwala, granted free discharge 1.2.51
2387	Pte.	SELBY William	C	-	Killed at Chilianwala
2274	Pte.	SEWELL Walter	C	G	Died 10.11.50
2499	Pte.	SHARP Hiram	C	-	Wounded at Chilianwala, invalided 28.8.50 to England 1.2.51
2693	Pte.	SHARP Joseph	C	-	Killed at Chilianwala
1399	Pte.	SHAW James	C	-	Killed at Chilianwala
2724	Pte.	SHEA Daniel	C	-	Killed at Chilianwala
3159	Pte.	SHEA Edmond	C	-	Killed at Chilianwala
2817	Pte.	SHEAN Thomas	C	G	Wounded at Chilianwala
1785	Cpl.	SHERRIFF James	C	-	Killed at Chilianwala
	Capt.	SHORE John S.	C	-	Killed at Chilianwala
2735	Pte.	SHORE Thomas	C	G	Wounded at Chilianwala
1932	Pte.	SIERS Walter	C	-	Killed at Chilianwala
2293	Pte.	SIMMONDS Joshua	C	G	Wounded at Chilianwala
3380	Pte.	SIMMONDS Daniel	C	-	Wounded at Chilianwala, invalided 6.2.49, to England 10.5.49
2475	Pte.	SIMMONDS William G.	C	-	Killed at Chilianwala
866	Pte.	SIMSON Charles	C	-	Killed at Chilianwala
1318	Pte.	SLADE John	C	G	Granted free discharge 1.2.51
1186	Pte.	SLADEN William	C	-	Killed at Chilianwala
2665	Pte.	SLATTERY James	C	-	Killed at Chilianwala
2435	Pte.	SLAUGHTER Henry	C	-	Wounded at Chilianwala
3123	Pte.	SMITH Charles	C	G	Wounded at Chilianwala
2055	Cpl.	SMITH Edward	C	-	Wounded at Chilianwala
2211	Pte.	SMITH George	C	G	Dead
3019	Pte.	SMITH George	C	-	Killed at Chilianwala
3129	Pte.	SMITH George Henry	C	-	Wounded at Chilianwala
2906	Pte.	SMITH Richard	C	-	Killed at Chilianwala
3144	Pte.	SMITH Samuel	C	-	Killed at Chilianwala
1786	Pte.	SMITH William	C	-	Killed at Chilianwala
1866	Pte.	SMITH William	C	G	Died 21.11.50
1364	Drummer	SMITH William	C	G	Free discharge 1.2.51
2993	Pte.	SNOOK William	C	-	Wounded at Chilianwala
2908	Pte.	SOMERSGILL John	C	-	Killed at Chilianwala
3142	Pte.	SOVAGHAN	C	-	Killed at Chilianwala
2127	Pte.	SPILLANE Maurice	C	-	Wounded at Chilianwala, died 19.8.50
	Lieut.	STANFORD Francis	-	G	Joined from 53rd Foot 2.7.49, died 5.9.49
	Lieut.	STEWART James	-	G	Joined from 98th Foot 14.2.49
1555	Sjt.	STOCKINGS James	C	G	Invalided 16.8.49, to England 16.2.50
2501	Pte.	STRUDWICK	C	-	Wounded at Chilianwala.
2002	Pte.	SUTHERLAND Alexander	C	-	Wounded at Chilianwala
2708	Pte.	SWEENEY Patrick	C	G	Wounded at Chilianwala
2498	Pte.	SYMONDS Thomas	C	G	Wounded at Chilianwala
2856	Pte.	TABBLE John	C	-	Killed at Chilianwala

2909	Pte.	TASKER Hiram	C	G	Wounded at Chilianwala
3162	Pte.	TAYLOR George	C	G	Wounded at Chilianwala
2212	Pte.	TAYLOR Joseph	C	-	Wounded at Chilianwala
3113	Pte.	TAYLOR William	C	G	Wounded at Chilianwala
2937	Pte.	TEMPLETON James	C	G	Died 7.9.49
1036	Pte.	TERRY John	C	-	Killed at Chilianwala
	Lieut.	THELWALL J.B.	C	G	Wounded at Chilianwala
3130	Pte.	THOMAS William	C	G	Died 7.6.49
1756	Sjt.	THOMPSON Charles	C	G	Wounded at Chilianwala
1351	Pte.	THOMPSON Richard	C	-	Wounded at Chilianwala
3138	Pte.	THOMPSON William	C	-	Killed at Chilianwala
1605	Pte.	TOBYN William	C	-	Killed at Chilianwala
1322	Pte.	TOMLIN John	C	G	Died 24.8.49
1762	Pte.	TOMLYN Charles	C	-	Wounded at Chilianwala
2910	Pte.	TONSON Daniel	C	G	Wounded at Chilianwala
2166	Pte.	TOWNEND James	C	-	Killed at Chilianwala
2523	Pte.	TOWNLEY William Samuel	C	-	Wounded at Chilianwala, invalided 4.9.49, to England 7.2.50
2794	Pte.	TOULEY James	C	-	Killed at Chilianwala
3008	Pte.	TOVEY George	C	G	Wounded at Chilianwala
2141	Pte.	TRACEY Patrick	C	G	Wounded at Chilianwala, died 29.6.49
	Lieut.	TRAVERS Richard H.	M	G	With 10th at Mooltan, with 24th 17.2.49
	Capt.	TRAVERS Robert William	C	-	Killed at Chilianwala
2605	Pte.	TRIMBLETT John	Medal only		Died 13.1.50
1668	Pte.	TROUBRIDGE William	C	-	Wounded at Chilianwala, died 11.12.49
2911	Pte.	TUMBER Edward	C	G	Wounded at Chilianwala, died 11.12.49
2964	Pte.	TURNER George	C	-	Wounded at Chilianwala
1331	Pte.	TURNER Henry	C	G	Granted free discharge 1.2.51
2195	Pte.	TURNER Henry	C	-	Wounded at Chilianwala
955	Pte.	TURNER John	-	G	Died 14.10.49
2338	Pte.	TWIGG Joshua	C	-	Killed at Chilianwala
2221	Pte.	TYDEMAN Henry	Medal only		Died 3.2.49
1200	Pte.	TYERS John	C	-	Killed at Chilianwala
2620	Pte.	URQUART John A.	C	G	Wounded at Chilianwala
3177	Pte.	VARDEN Patrick	C	G	Wounded at Chilianwala
2562	Pte.	WADE John	C	G	Wounded at Chilianwala
2912	Pte.	WAKEFIELD John	C	-	Killed at Chilianwala
3114	Pte.	WAKEMAN William	C	G	Wounded at Chilianwala
3147	Pte.	WALKER George	C	-	Wounded at Chilianwala
1712	Pte.	WALKER Joseph	C	-	Killed at Chilianwala
2529	Pte.	WALKER Samuel	C	G	Wounded at Chilianwala
3051	Pte.	WALKER William	C	-	Killed at Chilianwala
3157	Pte.	WALLIS William	C	G	Died 17.10.49
2808	Pte.	WALSH Patrick	C	G	Killed 7.10.50
2609	Pte.	WALSH William	C	-	Killed at Chilianwala
3117	Pte.	WARR James	C	G	Wounded at Chilianwala, invalided 25.8.50, to England 1.2.51

2913	Pte.	WARNER Edwin	C	-	Wounded at Chilianwala
3125	Pte.	WARREN James	C	-	Killed at Chilianwala
2916	Pte.	WARREN Joseph	C	-	Wounded at Chilianwala
1342	Pte.	WARREN Robert	C	-	Wounded at Chilianwala, invalided 16.2.49, to England 10.5.49
2072	Cpl.	WEBB Henry	C	-	Killed at Chilianwala
2519	Pte.	WEBB Henry	C	G	Wounded at Chilianwala
2280	Pte.	WEBB John	C	G	Wounded at Chilianwala
1579	Sjt.	WEBSTER John	C	-	Killed at Chilianwala
	Ensign.	WEDDERBURN George	-	G	From 53rd 10.2.49, and 24th 20.10.49
2761	Pte.	WEIGHTMAN Henry	C	-	Killed at Chilianwala
3040	Pte.	WELCH John	C	-	Killed at Chilianwala
1207	Pte.	WELDON Alfred	C	-	Killed at Chilianwala
1304	Cpl.	WELHAM George	C	G	Free discharge to 1st European Regt. 7.7.49
2799	Pte.	WELTON Benjamin	C	-	Wounded at Chilianwala
3168	Pte.	WELTON William	C	-	Killed at Chilianwala
1011	Pte.	WEST James	C	G	Died 25.11.50
2631	Pte.	WEST William	C	-	Wounded at Chilianwala, invalided 12.9.50, to England 23.2.51
1242	Pte.	WESTNEAT Peter	C	-	Killed at Chilianwala
2667	Pte.	WETHERSPOON William	C	G	Wounded at Chilianwala
2348	Pte.	WEYBOURNE Edward	C	G	Wounded at Chilianwala
1306	Cpl.	WHALES James	C	-	Wounded at Chilianwala
2915	Pte.	WHEATON George	C	G	Wounded at Chilianwala, died 4.10.50
2171	Pte.	WHEELER Daniel	C	-	Killed at Chilianwala
2275	Pte.	WHITE John	C	G	Wounded at Chilianwala
3015	Pte.	WHITE Richard	C	G	Wounded at Chilianwala
2933	Pte.	WHITEHEAD Charles	C	O	Killed at Chilianwala
1310	Pte.	WHITTAKER James	C	G	Wounded at Chilianwala
895	Pte.	WHITTELL Ambrose	C	-	Killed at Chilianwala
1999	Cpl.	WILKS John	C	-	Killed at Chilianwala
2110	Pte.	WILLIAMS Edward	C	-	Wounded at Chilianwala
	Lieut.	WILLIAMS George E.L.	C	-	Wounded at Chilianwala. Capt. 14.1.49
2448	Pte.	WILLIAMS James	C	-	Killed at Chilianwala
3174	Pte.	WILLIAMS John	C	G	Wounded at Chilianwala
2140	Pte.	WILLIAMS William	C	-	Wounded at Chilianwala
2088	Pte.	WILLIS William	C	-	Killed at Chilianwala
2182	Pte.	WILLIS William	C	G	Wounded at Chilianwala
2252	Pte.	WILLSON George	C	-	Wounded at Chilianwala
1348	Sjt.	WILMOTT Charles	-	G	Sent home on free discharge 1.2.51
2086	Pte.	WILSON Christopher	C	-	Wounded at Chilianwala, invalided 4.9.49, to England 7.2.50
2456	Pte.	WHITEROD James	C	-	Wounded at Chilianwala
2551	Pte.	WILSON Robert	C	G	Wounded at Chilianwala
2527	Pte.	WINDLE Richard	C	-	Killed at Chilianwala
1168	Pte.	WINDLE William	C	G	Died 9.1.51
1096	Pte.	WOOD John	C	-	Killed at Chilianwala

24th Foot continued

	Lieut.	WOODGATE James A.	C	-	Killed at Chilianwala
	Lieut.	WOODINGTON H.P.T.	C	G	Resigned. Sale of commission 15.11.49
1182	Pte.	WOODINGTON Thomas W.	C	-	Wounded at Chilianwala, invalided 4.9.49, to England 7.2.50
1496	Pte.	WORLEY Charles	C	-	Killed at Chilianwala
2203	Cpl.	YARD John	C	G	Wounded at Chilianwala
2431	Pte.	YATES Thomas	C	G	Died 6.12.50
2688	Pte.	YOUNG William	Medal only		Died of wounds received atSadoolapore 8.12.48
1989	Sjt.	BURTON John	C	G	Wounded at Chilianwala

* * *

29th FOOT

2169	Pte.	ADDICOTT Charles	C	G	Wounded at Chilianwala
1507	Pte.	ADDICOTT George	C	G	Invalided 22.8.49, to England 1.3.50
1879	Pte.	AILL James W.	C	G	Died 15.9.49
2856	Pte.	ALLISON Edward	C	G	Died 7.3.50
2667	Pte.	AMEY Uriah	C	G	Wounded at Chilianwala
2648	Pte.	ANDERSON Isaac	C	-	Wounded at Chilianwala, invalided 27.8.50, to England 26.2.51
1808	Pte.	ANDERSON Robert	C	G	Died 6.10.49
2386	Pte.	ANDREWS Henry	C	G	Wounded at Chilianwala, died 29.10.49
2733	Pte.	ANDREWS Samuel	C	G	Died 28.8.49
679	Sjt.	ARMSTRONG John	C	G	Invalided 22.8.49, to England 1.3.50
992	Pte.	ASH George	C	G	Died 19.4.49
2641	Pte.	BACON James	C	G	Died 13.8.49
2790	Pte.	BADGER George	C	-	Wounded at Chilianwala
1811	Pte.	BADMAN James	C	G	Wounded at Chilianwala
1876	Pte.	BAGWORTH Thomas	C	G	Invalided 22.8.49, to England 1.3.50
2960	Cpl.	BAILEY Thomas	C	G	Died 28.10.49
589	ORC Clr.Sjt.	BAMPTON John	C	G	Invalided 27.8.50, to England 26.2.51
1608	Pte.	BARKER William	C	G	Discharged by purchase 23.10.50
2133	Pte.	BARRETT William	C	-	Wounded at Chilianwala
2223	Pte.	BARRY Richard	C	G	Wounded at Chilianwala
2300	Pte.	BASFORD Walter	C	G	Wounded at Chilianwala
2859	Pte.	BAXTER John	-	-	Died 27.11.48
2199	Pte.	BEAL Alexander	C	G	Died 16.4.49
1836	Pte.	BEASLEY John	C	-	Wounded at Chilianwala, invalided 7.2.49, to England 10.5.49
967	Pte.	BEECH Richard	C	-	Killed at Chilianwala
1013	Pte.	BEGLEY Andrew	-	G	Invalided 27.8.50, to England 12.3.51
1873	Pte.	BENSON Albert	-	-	Died 11.12.48
2163	Pte.	BENTLEY John	C	G	Wounded at Chilianwala
2920	Pte.	BIGGS Alfred	-	-	Died 8.1.49
1831	Pte.	BLAIN James	C	G	Invalided 22.8.49, to England 1.3.50
2630	Pte.	BLAKE Richard	C	-	Wounded at Chilianwala, invalided 4.9.49, to England 7.2.50
2610	Pte.	BLAKES Joseph	C	G	Died 23.12.50
983	Sjt.	BOOTH Samuel	C	-	Died 2.4.49

1504	Cpl.	BOULDING Robert	C	G	Wounded at Chilianwala
2009	Pte.	BOYCE William	C	G	Wounded at Chilianwala, discharge by purchase 12.2.51
2827	Pte.	BOYLEN Owen	C	G	Died 14.9.50
1517	Pte.	BRADFORD John	C	G	Invalided 22.8.49, to England 1.3.50
2968	Pte.	BRADLEY John	C	G	Wounded at Chilianwala
2504	Pte.	BRADY Lawrence	C	-	Wounded at Chilianwala, invalided 27.8.49 to England 1.3.51
2865	Pte.	BRANCH William	C	G	Invalided 27.8.50, to England 26.2.51
2753	Pte.	BREEN Charles	C	G	Wounded at Chilianwala
2824	Pte.	BRICE Thomas	C	G	Wounded at Chilianwala
2525	Pte.	BRODERICK Thomas	C	G	Dead
1964	Sjt.	BROOKS George	C	-	Wounded at Chilianwala, invalided 27.8.49 to England 1.3.50
663	Pte.	BROWN Andrew	C	-	Died of wounds received at Chilianwala 20.1.49
1902	Pte.	BROWN William	C	G	Wounded at Chilianwala, discharged by purchase 16.10.50
2048	Cpl.	BRYAN Michael	C	G	Invalided 22.8.49, to England 1.3.50
1267	Pte.	BUCKLEY Charles	C	-	Killed at Chilianwala
2179	Pte.	BULGER John	-	-	Died 21.11.48
2243	Pte.	BUNTING Thomas	C	-	Killed at Chilianwala
2065	Pte.	BURGESS James	C	G	Wounded at Chilianwala
1922	Pte.	BURKE James	C	G	Wounded at Chilianwala
1699	Pte.	BURNS James	C	-	Wounded at Chilianwala, invalided 28.8.50, to England 26.2.51
1066	Pte.	BUTT John	C	G	Invalided 22.8.49, to England 1.3.50
1893	Pte.	BYE Charles	C	G	Died 24.7.50
2634	Pte.	BYRNE John	C	G	Wounded at Chilianwala
1910	Pte.	CALANAN Daniel	C	G	Died 9.12.50
1670	Pte.	CAMMACK Thomas	C	G	Wounded at Chilianwala
1697	Pte.	CAMPBELL James	C	-	Killed at Chilianwala
2898	Pte.	CAMPBELL John	-	-	Died 3.1.49
1909	Sjt.	CAREY Patrick	C	-	Killed at Chilianwala
2477	Pte.	CARR William	C	-	Wounded at Chilianwala
2250	Pte.	CARROLL John	C	G	Wounded at Chilianwala
2621	Pte.	CARROLL John	C	-	Invalided 4.9.49, to England 7.2.50
2206	Pte.	CARTHY John	C	G	Died 9.7.49
2274	Pte.	CATHY George	C	-	Died of wounds received at Chilianwala 14.1.49
2512	Pte.	CAULFIELD George	C	-	Wounded at Chilianwala, invalided 4.9.49, to England 7.2.50
2047	Pte.	CAYS Denis	C	G	Died 3.9.49
1459	Pte.	CHAPPELL Robert	C	G	Died 20.8.50
1966	Pte.	CHASE John	C	G	Died 31.12.49
2919	Pte.	CHIVERS William	C	G	Wounded at Goojerat
1970	Pte.	CHURCHER William	-	-	Died 7.12.48
2890	Pte.	CLARKE William	C	-	Died 17.2.49
2662	Pte.	CLIFT Henry	C	G	Died 17.10.49
2242	Pte.	COFFEE Michael	C	-	Wounded at Chilianwala, invalided 7.2.49 to England 10.5.49

29th Foot continued

No.	Rank	Name			Remarks
2350	Pte.	COLK John	C	G	Invalided 27.8.50, to England 26.2.51
2660	Pte.	COMBS Phillip	C	-	Died 25.3.49
2776	Pte.	CONNELL Peter	C	G	Discharge by purchase 26.9.49
855	Pte.	CONNOR John	C	G	Wounded at Chilianwala
2489	Pte.	CONROY Richard	C	-	Wounded at Chilianwala, died 20.2.50
2454	Pte.	COOKE James C.	C	G	Died 28.9.49
2019	Pte.	COONEY Edmund	C	-	Killed at Chilianwala
787	Pte.	COTTER Matthew	C	G	Invalided 22.8.49, to England 1.3.50
2794	Pte.	COTTER Pierce	C	-	Killed at Chilianwala
1609	Cpl.	COUBROUGH Robert	C	G	Wounded at Chilianwala, invalided 27.8.50, to England 26.2.51
942	Pte.	COUGHLAN Michael	C	G	Died 21.7.49
2316	Pte.	CRAMPTON John	C	G	Dead
2757	Pte.	CREAGHAN Lawrence	C	G	Wounded at Chilianwala
1329	Pte.	CREAKE Samuel	C	G	Invalided 22.8.49, to England 1.3.50
2787	Pte.	CRIMEN Patrick	-	-	Died 21.11.48
1948	Pte.	CROSSLEY John	C	G	Wounded at Chilianwala
988	Pte.	CROWLEY John	C	G	Wounded at Chilianwala, invalided 27.8.50, to England 26.2.51
1560	Pte.	CULLEN John	C	G	Wounded at Chilianwala, discharge by purchase 30.3.50
1743	Pte.	DAILY Bernard	C	-	Killed at Chilianwala
1514	Pte.	DAISLEY James	C	G	Wounded at Goojerat
2413	Pte.	DANIELS Edward R.	C	G	Wounded at Chilianwala
1227	Pte.	DARMON Joseph	C	-	Killed at Chilianwala
2775	Pte.	DAVIS James	C	G	Wounded at Chilianwala
1820	Pte.	DAWKINS Henry	C	-	Killed at Chilianwala
2876	Pte.	DEMPSEY Patrick	C	-	Killed at Chilianwala
2193	Pte.	DEMPSEY Timothy	C	-	Died 15.3.49
1223	Pte.	DENNIS John	C	G	Wounded at Chilianwala
2977	Pte.	DERWAN William	C	G	Died 14.11.50
1204	Pte.	DICKINSON Henry	C	G	Wounded at Chilianwala, died 1.5.49
2748	Pte.	DONAHAN Patrick	C	-	Wounded at Chilianwala
2732	Pte.	DONOVAN John (2)	C	-	Killed at Chilianwala
2435	Cpl.	DOOLEY Charles	-	G	Died 12.2.50
2853	Sjt.	DOUBLE John	C	G	Invalided 22.6.49, permitted to reside in India
2692	Pte.	DOUGLAS Edward	-	-	Died 17.12.48
1602	Clr.Sjt.	DOUGLAS George	C	G	Invalided 27.8.50, to England 26.2.51
2672	Pte.	DOWN Robert	C	G	Died 5.5.49
2902	Pte.	DOWNES Peter	C	G	Wounded at Chilianwala
1908	Pte.	DOWNES Yearly	C	-	Wounded at Chilianwala, died 13.9.49
1026	Clr.Sjt.	DOWNIE Thomas	C	G	Discharge by purchase 26.9.49
2765	Pte.	DRISCOLL John	C	-	Wounded at Chilianwala, died 22.11.50
1727	Pte.	DUNLOP John (1)	C	-	Died of wounds received at Chilianwala 27.1.49
2532	Pte.	DUNNE Alexander	C	-	Died of wounds received at Chilianwala 20.1.49
2576	Pte.	DUNNE Martin	C	-	Wounded at Chilianwala, died 18.2.49
996	Pte.	DUTTON Ebenezer	C	-	Died 3.2.49
1962	Pte.	EDWARDS Jonathan	C	G	Wounded at Chilianwala

1694	Pte.	ELLIOTT Thomas	C	-	Died 26.8.49
2791	Pte.	ELSOM William	C	G	Died 5.7.49
1799	Pte.	ELSWORTH David	C	-	Died 8.2.49
2484	Pte.	EVERETT John	C	G	Wounded at Chilianwala
2905	Pte.	FAHY Martin	C	-	Wounded at Chilianwala, invalided 7.2.49, to England 10.5.49
2896	Pte.	FANNON Phillip	-	-	Died 25.8.49
2609	Pte.	FARNOLL John	C	-	Killed at Chilianwala
2434	Pte.	FEARON Patrick	C	G	Died 3.5.50
2471	Pte.	FEEGAN Henry	C	-	Wounded at Chilianwala, invalided 4.9.49, to England 7.2.50
1638	Pte.	FEY John	C	G	Wounded at Chilianwala
2981	Pte.	FEY James	-	-	Died 6.6.49
2013	Pte.	FIDLER Job	C	-	Killed at Chilianwala
831	Sjt.	FIELD George	C	G	Died 21.8.49
705	Pte.	FINNIMORE William	C	G	Invalided 22.8.49, to England 1.3.50
2752	Pte.	FITZGERALD Michael	-	-	Died 16.12.48
2718	Pte.	FITZPATRICK James	C	G	Died 2.6.49
2221	Pte.	FITZPATRICK Moses	C	G	Invalided 22.8.49, to England 1.3.50
2783	Pte.	FLANNAGAN Lawrence	C	G	Wounded at Chilianwala, died 27.9.50
2679	Drummer	FLEMING John	C	-	Wounded at Chilianwala, invalided 4.9.49, to England 7.2.50
2730	Pte.	FLEMING Samuel	C	-	Wounded at Chilianwala, invalided 27.8.49, to England 1.3.50
2680	Pte.	FLEMING William	C	G	Wounded at Chilianwala
838	Pte.	FLEOH Patrick	C	G	Died 11.6.49
2970	Pte.	FOLEY John	C	G	Died 6.11.49
2230	Pte.	FORTH John	C	G	With 24th Foot at Goojerat, died 1.9.50
1538	Pte.	FOSTER Henry	C	-	Wounded at Chilianwala, invalided 4.9.49, to England 7.2.50
2308	Drummer	FOWLES Richard	C	-	Wounded at Chilianwala
1316	Pte.	FRANCIS Charles	-	-	Died 29.11.48
2907	Pte.	FRANCIS Solomon	C	-	Died 25.1.49
	Capt.	FRASER Aneas	-	-	Died 29.4.49
1783	Pte.	FRAZER John	C	-	Wounded at Chilianwala, invalided 27.8.49, to England 1.3.50
2962	Pte.	FUNSTON Andrew	C	-	Died 6.5.49
2458	Pte.	FURZE James O.	C	G	Invalided 27.8.50, to England 26.2.51
144	Pte.	GARDINER James	C	G	Wounded at Chilianwala, invalided 27.8.49, to England 1.3.50
1715	Pte.	GIBSON John	C	G	Killed at Goojerat
1534	Sjt.	GILBY Joseph	-	-	Died 27.1.49
1926	Pte.	GILES William	C	-	Killed at Chilianwala
1607	Pte.	GILLON William	C	G	Wounded at Chilianwala
1059	Pte.	GODFREY William	C	-	Died 4.2.49
2099	Pte.	GODING Francis	C	G	Invalided 22.8.49, to England 1.3.50
2252	Pte.	GOODING John	-	-	Died 16.3.49
962	Pte.	GOODWIN Simeon	C	G	Invalided 27.8.50, to England 26.2.51
2720	Pte.	GOSTILER John	C	-	Killed at Chilianwala
1440	Pte.	GOUGH Thomas	C	G	Wounded at Chilianwala

29th Foot continued

1993	Pte.	GRAY William	C	G	Wounded at Chilianwala
2480	Drummer	GREER John	C	G	Wounded at Chilianwala
2663	Pte.	GRIFFIN John	C	G	Wounded at Chilianwala
2734	Pte.	GRIMES Patrick	C	G	Drowned 31.7.49
802	Pte.	GUEST Frederick	C	-	Killed at Chilianwala
2162	Pte.	GUMMER Jacob	C	-	Wounded at Chilianwala
2595	Pte.	HACKETT James	C	-	Wounded at Chilianwala
1533	Pte.	HADFIELD Michael	C	-	Died of wounds received at Chilianwala 15.1.49
2120	Pte.	HAGAN James	C	G	Wounded at Chilianwala
2702	Pte.	HAGARTY John	C	G	Wounded at Chilianwala
2257	Pte.	HAGGETT George	C	-	Killed at Chilianwala
1104	Pte.	HALFORD John	C	G	Wounded at Chilianwala
2166	Pte.	HALL John	C	G	Invalided 22.8.49, to England 1.3.50
1219	Pte.	HALLERAN Dennis	C	G	Wounded at Chilianwala
2974	Pte.	HAMILTON Thomas	C	G	Wounded at Chilianwala, died 7.9.49
1592	Pte.	HANSFORD George	C	G	Wounded at Chilianwala
2699	Pte.	HARDEMAN John	C	G	Died 30.6.49
1233	Pte.	HARDEMAN Solomon	C	-	Died of wounds received at Chilianwala 11.4.49
1083	Cpl.	HARDWICK William	-	-	Died 28.1.49
1711	Cpl.	HARWOOD John	C	-	Wounded at Chilianwala, invalided 4.9.49, to England 7.2.50
1828	Pte.	HATCH George	C	G	Wounded at Chilianwala, died 19.5.49
2401	Pte.	HAWKER Charles	C	G	Wounded at Chilianwala
1616	Sjt.	HAY William	C	G	Wounded at Chilianwala
2873	Pte.	HAZELL Robert	C	G	Died 1.11.49
2924	Pte.	HAZLE Thomas	C	-	Wounded at Chilianwala
2459	Pte.	HEELY William	C	-	Died 31.1.49
2774	Pte.	HEENAN Dennis	C	G	Wounded at Chilianwala
1390	Sjt.	HENRY William	-	-	Died 26.1.49
2194	Pte.	HIBBERT James	C	-	Wounded at Chilianwala, died 24.11.49
1832	Pte.	HICKLING Richard	C	G	Died 27.5.49
950	Cpl.	HIGGINS John	C	G	Wounded at Chilianwala
1620	Pte.	HINDLEY John	C	-	Wounded at Chilianwala, invalided 7.2.49, to England 10.5.49
2781	Pte.	HINDS Joseph	C	G	Died 29.6.50
1334	Pte.	HOBBS Charles	C	G	Invalided 27.8.50, to England 26.2.51
1286	Pte.	HODDER Robert	C	-	Died of wounds received at Chilianwala 20.1.49
2921	Pte.	HOFFAN John	C	-	Wounded at Chilianwala
2936	Pte.	HOGAN Michael	-	-	Died 22.11.48
1378	Pte.	HOLDING George	-	-	Invalided 27.8.49, to England 1.3.50
2079	Pte.	HOLLIDAY James	-	-	Died 8.5.49
2587	Pte.	HOLMES James	C	G	Dead
1524	Pte.	HOOKWAY David	C	G	Wounded at Chilianwala, invalided 27.8.50, to England 26.12.51
2511	Pte.	HOOPER John	C	-	Died of wounds received at Chilianwala 15.1.49
1509	Pte.	HOOPER William	C	G	Wounded at Chilianwala
2487	Pte.	HOPKINS Abraham	C	G	Died 9.9.49
2443	Pte.	HOPKINS Michael	C	-	Killed at Chilianwala

2427	Pte.	HORAN Michael	-	-	Died 28.11.48
1469	Sjt.	HOWELL Samuel	C	G	Wounded at Chilianwala
2421	Pte.	HUBBARD Charles	C	G	Wounded at Goojerat
2510	Pte.	HUDDY George	C	G	Died 17.12.49
2146	Pte.	HUGGINS William	C	G	Wounded at Chilianwala
2370	Pte.	HUGHES John	C	G	Wounded at Chilianwala
1114	Cpl.	HUGES Thomas	C	G	Wounded at Chilianwala
2588	Pte.	HUMPHREYS Ebenezer	-	-	Died 19.12.48
2364	Pte.	HUSSEY John	C	-	Killed at Chilianwala
2373	Pte.	HUTCHINS Edmund	C	G	Died 26.9.49
2600	Pte.	INDOA James	C	G	Wounded at Chilianwala
2126	Pte.	INGLES Jesse	C	G	Wounded at Chilianwala
1734	Pte.	IRELAND William J.	C	-	Wounded at Chilianwala
1542	Pte.	ISHERWOOD James	C	G	Died 11.4.49
2535	Pte.	JACKSON William	C	G	Wounded at Chilianwala
2563	Pte.	JACQUES John	C	G	Died 23.6.49
2682	Pte.	JENKINS William (2)	C	-	Killed at Chilianwala
2604	Pte.	JEWELL John	C	-	Wounded at Chilianwala
1053	Pte.	JONES Ezekiel	C	-	Wounded at Chilianwala, invalided 27.8.49, to England 1.3.50
1430	Pte.	JONES John (1)	C	G	Wounded at Chilianwala
2470	Pte.	JONES John (2)	C	-	Wounded at Chilianwala
2129	Pte.	JONES William	C	-	Wounded at Chilianwala, invalided 4.9.49, to England 7.2.50
2966	Pte.	JOYCE John	C	G	Died 1.8.49
2376	Pte.	JUDGE James	C	-	Wounded at Chilianwala, invalided 27.8.49, to England 1.3.50
2694	Pte.	JUDGE Joseph	C	-	Wounded at Chilianwala, invalided 4.9.49, to England 7.2.50
2414	Pte.	KAIN James	C	G	Wounded at Goojerat
2779	Pte.	KAIN Thomas	C	G	Wounded at Chilianwala, died 9.4.49
2408	Pte.	KEAN John	C	G	Invalided 27.8.50, to England 26.2.51
1683	Drummer	KEARNES John	C	-	Wounded at Chilianwala
1662	Cpl.	KEARNEY William	C	G	Invalided 22.8.49, to England 1.3.50
2298	Pte.	KEMBLE Richard	C	G	Died 8.11.50
1914	Pte.	KEMP Joseph	C	G	Wounded at Chilianwala
2761	Pte.	KENNEDY Michael	C	-	Wounded at Chilianwala, invalided 4.9.49, to England 7.2.50
2834	Pte.	KENNELL Thomas	C	-	Died of wounds received at Chilianwala 18.1.49
2842	Pte.	KENNEFICK William	C	G	Died 14.3.49
2464	Pte.	KEOGAN Patrick	C	G	Wounded at Chilianwala, invalided 27.8.50, to England 26.2.51
1589	Pte.	KERR David	C	G	Died 27.6.50
2029	Cpl.	KERSHAW Henry	C	G	Wounded at Goojerat
2599	Pte.	KNIGHT Richard	C	G	Wounded at Chilianwala
2852	Pte.	KYLE William	C	G	Invalided 27.8.50, to England 26.2.51
2097	Pte.	LENDEN Charles	C	G	Died 31.7.49
2668	Pte.	LEWIS Charles	C	G	Died 14.5.49
2572	Pte.	LEWIS James	C	-	Wounded at Chilianwala, invalided 27.8.49, to England 1.3.50

2799	Pte.	LILLIS Patrick	-	-	Died 30.11.48
1768	Pte.	LINES William	C	-	Wounded at Chilianwala, invalided 7.2.49, to England 10.5.49
1717	Pte.	LITTLEWOOD John	C	G	Died 31.8.50
2404	Pte.	LIVINGSTON Samuel	C	G	Wounded at Chilianwala
2690	Pte.	LONG Daniel	C	G	Wounded at Chilianwala
1870	Sjt.	LONG Robert	C	-	Killed at Chilianwala
1023	Pte.	LOWE George	C	G	Wounded at Chilianwala
1779	Pte.	LOWRIE William	C	G	Died 24.9.50
1271	Pte.	LOYNS John	C	G	Died 13.9.49
2623	Pte.	LUBY James	C	-	Wounded at Chilianwala, invalided 27.8.49, to England 1.3.50
646	Pte.	McANIFF Bartholomew	C	G	Invalided 22.8.49, to England 1.3.50
496	Sjt.	McBRIEN John	C	G	Invalided 12.8.50, permitted to reside in India
2046	Pte.	McCANN John	C	-	Wounded at Chilianwala, invalided 4.9.49, to England 7.2.50
2931	Pte.	McCANNERY Michael	C	G.	Wounded at Chilianwala
1289	Pte.	McCOOEY John	C	G	Died 12.4.49
2067	Pte.	McCORMICK William	C	G	Died 8.8.50
1698	Drummer	McCULLOUCH William	C	G	Invalided 22.8.49, to England 1.3.50
2180	Pte.	McDERMOTT Dominick	C	-	Killed at Chilianwala
2624	Pte.	McDONALD Henry	-	-	Died 22.5.49
1778	Pte.	McDOWELL George	C	G	Wounded at Chilianwala
2222	Pte.	McDOWELL James	C	G	Wounded at Chilianwala
876	Pte.	McGENNIS John	C	G	Invalided 22.8.49, to England 1.3.50
2428	Pte.	McGLAUGHLIN Charles	C	-	Killed at Chilianwala
1759	Pte.	McGLAUGHLIN Hugh	C	G	Wounded at Chilianwala
2446	Pte.	McGLAUGHLIN Martin	C	G	Died 27.4.50
2405	Pte.	McGLAUGHLIN Thomas	C	G	Wounded at Chilianwala
784	Pte.	McGUIGGAN	-	G	Invalided 22.8.49, to England 1.3.50
782	Pte.	McGUIRE Arthur	C	G	Died 22.6.49
2516	Pte.	McNAMARA Charles	C	G	Wounded at Chilianwala
2538	Pte.	McNAMARA John	C	G	Dead
2973	Pte.	McSPADDEN John	C	G	Invalided 22.8.49, to England 1.3.50
2961	Pte.	MACKIN Peter	C	G	Discharge by Purchase 19.2.51
2780	Pte.	MADDEN Jeremiah	C	-	Died 21.8.50
2607	Pte.	MAHONEY Cornelius	C	-	Wounded at Chilianwala, invalided 7.2.49, to England 10.5.49
2437	Pte.	MALLARD Edward	-	-	Invalided 7.2.49, to England 10.5.49
2719	Pte.	MALLON Edward	C	G	Transported as a felon for life 7.9.50
2266	Cpl.	MALONE Martin	C	G	Invalided 22.8.49, permitted to reside in India
2188	Pte.	MANSFIELD George	C	G	Died 6.4.50
1082	Pte.	MARRIOTT Thomas	C	-	Killed at Chilianwala
1917	Pte.	MARSHALL William (1)	C	G	Wounded at Chilianwala
2770	Pte.	MARSON Joseph	C	G	Wounded at Chilianwala
1865	Cpl.	MARTINE James	C	-	Wounded at Chilianwala, invalided 4.9.49, to England 7.2.50
2584	Pte.	MATHESION James	C	-	Wounded at Chilianwala
2693	Pte.	MAYHEW Joseph	C	-	Wounded at Chilianwala
2548	Pte.	MAY James	-	G	Invalided 27.8.50, to England 26.2.51

2946	Pte.	MAYO James	C	-	Killed at Chilianwala
	Lieut.	METGE Henry T.	C	-	Died of wounds 18.1.49
1807	Pte.	MIDDLETON Thomas	-	-	Died 30.11.48
2328	Pte.	MILLIAR Richard	C	G	Died 4.8.49
2608	Pte.	MILLS John	C	G	Died 24.5.49
681	Pte.	MILLS Thomas	C	G	Wounded at Chilianwala, invalided 22.8.49, to England 1.3.50
2914	Pte.	MILLSOM John	C	G	Invalided 22.8.49, to England 1.3.50
1000	Cpl.	MITCHELL John	C	G	Died 23.10.49
2755	Pte.	MONAHAN James	C	G	Wounded at Chilianwala, invalided 22.8.49, to England 1.3.50
	Capt. Hon.	MONKTON Horace M.	C	G	Wounded at Chilianwala
2549	Pte.	MORRISS Matthew	-	-	Died 15.11.48
2885	Pte.	MORRISON John	C	G	Wounded at Chilianwala
1641	Pte.	MOSS John	C	-	Wounded at Chilianwala, invalided 27.8.49, to England 1.3.50
	Lieut.	MOWBRAY Alexander R.	C	G	With 24th Foot at Goojerat, died 16.2.50
1816	Pte.	MULCAHY Patrick	C	-	Died 6.7.49
2351	Pte.	MULLEN Henry	C	G	Wounded at Chilianwala
1940	Pte.	MULLIN Thomas	C	-	Killed at Chilianwala
1728	Pte.	MURRAY James (1)	C	G	Wounded at Chilianwala, died 9.11.49
2064	Pte.	MURRAY James (2)	C	G	Wounded at Chilianwala
2756	Pte.	MURRAY John (2)	C	G	Wounded at Chilianwala
2839	Pte.	MURPHY Lawrence	C	G	Died 6.11.50
2406	Pte.	MURPHY William	C	-	Wounded at Chilianwala
2861	Pte.	MURTER Charles	C	G	Died 10.12.50
2860	Pte.	MURTER William	C	G	Died 5.11.49
1280	Pte.	MYERS Arthur	C	G	Discharged by purchase 26.9.49
1994	Pte.	NASH George	C	G	Wounded at Chilianwala
1522	Pte.	NAYLOR William	C	-	Killed at Chilianwala
2313	Pte.	NEAL Hugh	C	G	Died 12.9.49
2320	Pte.	NEAL Robert	C	G	Invalided 27.8.50, to England 26.2.51
1466	Pte.	NESBITT John	C	G	Wounded at Chilianwala
2875	Pte.	NEVARD Robert	C	-	Died 20.2.49
	Ensign.	NEVILL George H.	C	G	Wounded at Chilianwala
2661	Pte.	NEWCOMB William	C	G	Wounded at Chilianwala
1569	Pte.	NICHOLS Emanuel	C	G	Wounded at Chilianwala, died 26.8.49
1018	Cpl.	NICHOLSON Thomas	C	G	Wounded at Chilianwala, died 3.8.50
2938	Pte.	NIHILL Patrick	C	G	Dead
1672	Pte.	NORMAN Edmund	C	G	Wounded at Chilianwala
2785	Pte.	NORRIS Henry	C	-	Wounded at Chilianwala, died 5.10.49
2429	Pte.	O'DWIRE Michael	C	G	Died 7.2.51
2269	Cpl.	O'KEEFE Arther	C	G	Wounded at Chilianwala, discharged by purchase 28.9.50
2710	Pte.	OLIVER George	C	G	Wounded at Chilianwala
2806	Pte.	OLIVER Samuel	C	G	Invalided 22.8.49, to England 1.3.50
2837	Pte.	O'NEILL John	C	G	Died 25.9.50
2546	Pte.	O'NEILL Michael	C	G	Invalided 22.8.49, to England 1.3.50
2479	Pte.	ORMROD Samuel	C	G	Died 17.5.49
2532	Pte.	O'ROURKE John	C	G	Dead

1370	Pte.	PARKER John	C	G	Wounded at Chilianwala
1372	Cpl.	PARKER Samuel	C	G	Died 7.6.50
2412	Cpl.	PARRY Richard	C	-	Wounded at Chilianwala
2502	Pte.	PART Stephen	-	-	Died 24.11.48
2592	Pte.	PARTRIDGE Herbert	C	G	Invalided 22.8.49, to England 1.3.50
2493	Pte.	PATRICK John	-	-	Died 5.2.50
2814	Pte.	PATSON William	C	G	Wounded at Chilianwala
2601	Pte.	PAULL John	C	G	Wounded at Chilianwala, died 2.9.50
2265	Pte.	PHILLIPS George	-	-	Died 18.4.51
1650	Pte.	PHILLIPS Henry	C	G	Died 22.8.49
2935	Pte.	PIERSON James	C	G	Wounded at Chilianwala
2894	Pte.	PIKE Daniel	C	G	Wounded at Chilianwala
2823	Pte.	POWDERLEY Peter	C	G	Wounded at Chilianwala
1935	Pte.	PRATER Charles	C	G	Wounded at Chilianwala, died 6.7.50
2887	Pte.	PRATT William	C	-	Killed at Chilianwala
1551	Pte.	PYMM Charles	C	G	Wounded at Chilianwala, invalided 4.9.49, to England 7.2.50
1328	Sjt.	QUINN Joseph	C	-	Invalided 27.8.50, to England 26.2.51
1626	Pte.	RAE John	C	-	Wounded at Chilianwala, died 14.11.50
2327	Pte.	REED George (2)	C	G	Wounded at Chilianwala
2325	Pte.	REED George	C	G	Invalided 22.8.49, to England 1.3.50
2343	Pte.	REEVES Edward	C	G	Wounded at Chilianwala
1528	Pte.	REEVES Henry	C	G	Invalided 27.8.50, to England 26.2.51
2354	Pte.	REEVES James	C	G	Wounded at Chilianwala
2581	Pte.	REID Charles	C	G	Wounded at Chilianwala
2534	Pte.	RICE Stephen	C	G	Wounded at Chilianwala
2326	Pte.	RICHARDS Benjamin	-	-	Died 3.12.48
1500	Pte.	RICHARDSON William	C	G	Dead
2303	Pte.	RILEY Thomas	C	G	Wounded at Chilianwala
1595	Pte.	ROBERTS Andrew	C	G	Wounded at Chilianwala
2378	Pte.	ROBERTS William	C	G	Died 26.2.51
2337	Pte.	RORKE Peter	C	G	Died 11.6.49
2291	Pte.	ROURKE Andrew	C	G	Discharge by purchase 16.8.51
2033	Pte.	ROWLANDS George	-	-	Died 21.1.49
2886	Pte.	RUSSELL Daniel	C	G	Died 9.6.49
2491	Pte.	RYDER James	C	G	Wounded at Chilianwala
1367	Sjt.	SAUNDERS Henry	-	-	Invalided 27.8.50, to England 26.2.51
2906	Pte.	SAUNDERS James	-	-	Died 15.10.49
2700	Pte.	SHARP Alexander	C	G	Died 6.5.49
1930	Pte.	SHARP John	C	G	Died 12.6.50
2518	Pte.	SHEAN Patrick	C	G	Wounded at Chilianwala
2529	Pte.	SHENTON James	C	-	Killed at Chilianwala
2745	Pte.	SHERIDAN John	C	G	Invalided 22.8.49, to England 1.3.50
1217	Clr.Sjt.	SHIELLS William	C	G	Died 14.5.50
1022	Pte.	SHORE John	C	G	Wounded at Chilianwala
1530	Sjt.	SHUFFLEBOTHAM James	C	G	Died 29.10.50

No.	Rank	Name			Remarks
1612	Cpl.	SILVER James	C	G	Died 19.3.49
800	Drummer.	SKEFFINGTON John	C	G	Died 19.12.49
2513	Pte.	SMALL Hugh	C	-	Died of wounds received at Chilianwala 16.4.49
2681	Pte.	SMART Henry	C	-	Died of wounds received at Chilianwala 15.1.49
1206	Clr.Sjt.	SMITH Abel	C	G	Wounded at Chilianwala
	Major	SMITH Mathew	C	G	Wounded at Chilianwala, commanded 24th Foot at Goojerat.
2310	Pte.	SMITH Patrick	C	-	Wounded at Chilianwala
1614	Pte.	SMITH Robert	C	G	Invalided 22.8.49, to England 1.3.50
	Lieut.	SMITH William L.D.	C	G	Died 29.11.49
2854	Pte.	SMYTH John	C	G	Died 7.9.49
2978	Pte.	SMYTH Joseph	C	G	Died 22.5.51
2342	Pte.	SOMERS George	C	G	Invalided 27.8.50, to England 26.2.51
2465	Pte.	SOUTER Henry	C	-	Died of wounds received at Chilianwala 18.1.49
1875	Pte.	SQUIRE William	C	G	Wounded at Chilianwala
2142	Pte.	STACY John	C	G	Wounded at Chilianwala, died 27.8.49
1998	Pte.	STANBROOK David	C	G	Died 24.9.50
2348	Pte.	STEVENS John	C	-	Wounded at Chilianwala, invalided 27.8.49, to England 1.3.50
2488	Pte.	STOW John	C	G	Discharge by purchase 28.9.51
1168	Pte.	SULLIVAN Denis	C	G	Wounded at Chilianwala
2583	Pte.	SULLIVAN John (2)	C	G	Killed at Goojerat
680	Pte.	SUNLAY Edward	C	G	Invalided 22.8.49, to England 1.3.50
2358	Pte.	TANNER John	C	-	Died 19.2.49
719	Pte.	TAYLOR Benjamin	C	-	Wounded at Chilianwala, invalided 4.9.49, to England 7.2.50
2271	Cpl.	TAYLOR George	C	-	Died of wounds received at Chilianwala 21.1.49
2374	Pte.	TAYLOR Jonas	C	-	Killed at Chilianwala
2030	Pte.	TAYLOR Thomas (1)	C	-	Missing since 13.1.49
2904	Pte.	TAYLOR Thomas	C	G	Invalided 27.8.50, to England 26.2.51
1708	Pte.	THOMPSON John	C	G	Died 30.5.49
2002	Pte.	THORN Richard	C	G	Died 20.12.49
1989	Pte.	TIDBURY David	C	G	Wounded at Chilianwala
2749	Pte.	TOLE James	C	-	Wounded at Chilianwala, invalided 4.9.49, to England 7.2.50
2809	Pte.	TOWEY Michael	C	G	Wounded at Chilianwala, died 15.8.50
2357	Pte.	TRACEY Timothy	-	-	Died 22.8.49
1455	Clr.Sjt.	TRICKETT Thomas	C	G	Wounded at Chilianwala, invalided 22.8.49, to England 1.3.50
1418	Pte.	TURNER William	C	-	Died 13.2.49
2317	Pte.	TWAMBLEY John	C	-	Killed at Chilianwala
2869	Pte.	TYLEE George	C	G	Died 6.6.49
1287	Pte.	TYNAN Thomas	C	G	Wounded at Chilianwala, died 12.11.49
2490	Pte.	VORNEM Thomas	C	-	Missing since 13.1.49
1474	Pte.	VOWELLS James	C	-	Invalided 4.9.49, to England 7.2.50
2295	Pte.	WALDRON James	C	G	Invalided 22.8.49, to England 1.3.50
2844	Pte.	WALKER George	C	-	Wounded at Chilianwala, invalided 4.9.49, to England 7.2.50
2415	Pte.	WALKER Thomas	C	-	Killed at Chilianwala

1545	Pte.	WALSH John	C	G	Died 28.10.50
2811	Pte.	WALSH Mathew	C	G	Wounded at Chilianwala
954	Pte.	WALSH Thomas	C	-	Killed at Chilianwala
2506	Pte.	WARREN John	C	G	Wounded at Chilianwala, invalided 27.8.50, to England 26.2.51
2652	Pte.	WATTS Elisha	C	G	Wounded at Chilianwala
2282	Pte.	WEBBER William	C	G	Died 15.9.49
2571	Pte.	WHEALON Thomas	C	G	Discharge by purchase 7.5.51
1791	Pte.	WHITE John	C	G	Died 19.7.50
2645	Pte.	WHITE Robert	C	G	Wounded at Chilianwala
2631	Pte.	WHITE Thomas	C	G	Died 27.9.50
1611	Cpl.	WHITTAKER John	C	G	Wounded at Chilianwala
1485	Pte.	WILDBORE James	C	-	Killed at Chilianwala
2665	Pte.	WILKINS Thomas	C	-	Wounded at Chilianwala, invalided 7.2.49, to England 10.5.49
2338	Pte.	WILLIAMS Moses	C	G	Wounded at Chilianwala
776	Cpl.	WILLOUGHBY George	C	G	Invalided 28.8.59, to England 26.2.51
2863	Pte.	WILSON Nathan	C	G	Invalided 22.8.49, to England 1.3.50
1955	Pte.	WILSON William	C	G	Wounded at Chilianwala, invalided 22.8.49, to England 1.3.50
2499	Pte.	WILTSHIRE Charles	C	G	Wounded at Chilianwala
2893	Pte.	WINDER William	C	G	Wounded at Chilianwala
1960	Pte.	WITHERS John	-	-	Died 23.7.49
2430	Pte.	WOOD Robert (1)	C	-	Wounded at Chilianwala, died 30.6.49
2556	Pte.	WOODWARD George	C	G	Wounded at Chilianwala
1298	Pte.	WORTH William	C	G	Invalided 22.8.49, to England 1.3.50
2929	Pte.	WRAFF Joseph	C	G	Wounded at Chilianwala
2286	Pte.	WRIGHT Henry	C	G	Died 19.9.50
2331	Pte.	WYATT Benjamin	C	G	Wounded at Chilianwala
2052	Pte.	JARNELL Henry	C	G	Died 8.9.49
1782	Pte.	YOUNG Samuel	-	-	Died 5.1.49
1878	Sjt.	YOUNGMAN William	C	G	Died 23.11.49

* * *

32nd FOOT

3192	Pte.	ADAMSON Robert	M	G	Wounded at Goojerat 21.2.49
2513	Pte.	ADDISON James	M	G	Dead
3038	Pte.	AINDOW	M	-	Killed before Mooltan 6.11.48
3062	Pte.	ALEXANDER James	M	G	Wounded before Mooltan 6.11.48, died 25.8.49
2730	Pte.	ARNETT Patrick	M	G	Wounded before Mooltan 4.11.48, died 27.8.50
1657	Pte.	ASH James	M	-	Died 16.12.48
3036	Pte.	ASH William	M	-	Discharged 13.8.50
3193	Pte.	ASHE Thomas	Medal only		Died 31.7.48 en route to Mooltan
2241	Pte.	ATKINS Daniel	M	G	Dead
2794	Pte.	AYRES James	M	G	Transfered to 10th Foot 1.6.49
2772	Pte.	BAGHAN Michael	M	G	Died 17.7.49
1708	Pte.	BAILEY James	M	G	Wounded before Mooltan 12.9.48
	Capt.	BALFOUR Arthur L.	M	G	Wounded before Mooltan 12.9.48. Dead

3040	Pte.	BARLEY Joseph	M	G	Wounded before Mooltan 6.11.48
1639	Pte.	BARRACLOUGH Joseph	M	-	Wounded before Mooltan 12.9.48, discharged 13.8.50
2903	Pte.	BATT Edward	M	-	Wounded before Mooltan 12.9.48, discharged 9.10.49
1899	Cpl.	BEAUMONT Henry	Medal only		
2704	Cpl.	BEGGS Thomas	M	G	Discharge by purchase 21.10.50. To England
1523	Pte.	BIDDLE William	M	G	Died 5.6.50
3200	Pte.	BIRMINGHAM Henry	M	G	Transferred to 98th Foot 1.5.49
	Lieut.	BIRTWHISTLE William A.	M	G	Wounded before Mooltan 12.9.48
2633	Pte.	BLACK Edmund	M	G	Wounded before Mooltan 27.12.48
3064	Pte.	BLAKELY James	M	G	Died 22.2.50
2549	Pte.	BLCKEY James	M	G	Transfered to 98th Foot 1.6.50
540	Qtr.M.Sjt.	BLATCHFORD William	M	G	Died 31.3.49
1111	Pte.	BLISS Thomas	M	G	Died 26.5.50
1798	Pte.	BLOOD Thomas	M	G	Wounded before Mooltan 27.12.48
2900	Pte.	BODEL Robert	M	-	Killed before Mooltan 12.9.48
2626	Pte.	BOYHAN Patrick	M	G	Drowned 4.4.49
3043	Pte.	BRADLEY Joseph	M	-	Wounded before Mooltan 6.11.48, discharged 13.8.50
2986	Pte.	BRADY Daniel	M	G	Discharged 10.9.50
2728	Pte.	BRADY James	M	G	Transferred to 98th Foot 1.8.49
2664	Pte.	BRENTNALL Benjamin	Medal only		
1796	Pte.	BREWARD George	M	-	Died 13.1.49
2904	Cpl.	BRIARLY William	Medal only		Died 21.8.48 en route to Mooltan
1652	Pte.	BRICE Henry	M	G	Invalided 13.9.50, to England 1.2.51
2707	Pte.	BRICKNELL Samuel	M	-	Killed before Mooltan 6.11.48
	Capt.	BRINE Andrew G.	M	-	Wounded before Mooltan 16.1.49
2179	Pte.	BROWN John	M	G	Discharged by purchase 18.5.49, permitted to reside in India
1730	Sjt.	BROWNE Charles	M	-	Died 18.12.48
2776	Pte.	BURKE John	Medal only		
3209	Pte.	BURKE Thomas	M	G	Wounded before Mooltan 6.11.48
2845	Pte.	BURN Bernard	Medal only		
2125	Pte.	BURROW Henry	M	G	Drowned 14.3.50
3210	Pte.	BURROWS William	Medal only		Died 12.9.49
2968	Pte.	BUSBY James	M	G	Dead
1840	Pte.	BUTCHER Matthew	M	-	Died 28.11.48
2381	Pte.	BUTTERWORTH George	M	G	Wounded before Mooltan 2.1.49
1911	Pte.	BUXTON John	Medal only		Died 23.8.48 en route to Mooltan
1772	Pte.	CALF John	Medal only		Invalided. To rejoin.
2920	Clr.Sjt.	CAMPBELL James	M	G	Wounded before Mooltan 6.11.48
2906	Pte.	CAMPBELL James	M	G	Wounded before Mooltan 6.11.48
1665	Pte.	CANN George	M	G	Discharged by purchase 21.10.50. To England
3212	Pte.	CANNING Charles	Medal only		Died 11.8.48 en route to Mooltan
1509	Cpl.	CAPEL Thomas	M	G	Died 8.8.50
638	Pte.	CAREY John	M	G	Discharged 11.9.50
2586	Pte.	CARNES George	M	..	Wounded before Mooltan 12.9.48, discharged 24.9.52

32nd Foot continued

Medical subordinate
	Apothecary	CARRISON William G.	M	G	Invalided. Residing in India.
3017	Pte.	CARTER Edward	M	-	Killed before Mooltan 6.11.48
2930	Pte.	CHAPMAN Edward	M	G	Transfered to 87th Foot 1.9.50
1865	Pte.	CHATWIN Thomas	M	G	Discharge by purchase 21.10.50, to England
	Lieut.	CHIPPENDALL Edward	M	G	To 19th Regt. 2.11.49
	Major	CASE William	M	G	Wounded before Mooltan 27.12.48
2039	Pte.	CHURCH John	Medal only		Died 13.3.50
1791	Pte.	CHURCH John P.	M	-	Died 18.12.48
3151	Pte.	CLANCY Michael	M	-	Wounded before Mooltan 12.9.48. Discharged 26.6.49, permitted to reside in India, since gone to England
3215	Pte.	CLARKE Henry	M	G	Dischaged 10.9.50
1191	Pte.	CLARKE Thomas (1)	Medal only		Died 21.8.48 en route to Mooltan
2940	Pte.	CLARKE William	M	G	Wounded before Mooltan 2.1.49
3083	Pte.	CLEARY Joseph	M	-	Died 19.10.48
2669	Pte.	CLEAVES John	M	-	Died 21.1.49
2959	Pte.	COLES Joseph	M	-	Wounded before Mooltan 27.12.48
2488	Pte.	COLLIER John	Medal only		Drowned in River Sutley 11.8.48
2960	Pte.	COLLINS William	M	G	Discharged 10.9.50
3223	Pte.	CONNELL John	M	G	Wounded before Mooltan 27.12.48
2908	Pte.	CONNORS Michael	M	-	Died of wounds 11.11.48, received 6.11.48
3225	Pte.	CONNORS Patrick	M	G	Died 16.10.49
1987	Pte.	COTTLE John	M	-	Wounded before Mooltan 2.1.49
1817	Pte.	COX Edward	Medal only		Died 21.8.48 en route to Mooltan
3018	Pte.	COX John	M	G	Invalided 13.9.50. To England 1.2.51
2220	Pte.	CRANEY James	M	G	Died 5.10.49
3106	Pte.	CRANWELL William	M	G	Died 30.4.49
1795	Clr.Sjt.	CREECH Samuel B.	Medal only		Died 23.8.48 en route to Mooltan
3020	Pte.	CROWLEY Charles	M	G	Died 13.7.50
2034	Pte.	CULLEN Thomas	M	G	Died 25.7.49
3227	Pte.	CUMMINS John	M	G	Wounded before Mooltan 2.1.49
3228	Pte.	CURRY John	Medal only		
2124	Pte.	DASH James	M	G	Transferred to 22nd Foot 1.4.51
2560	Pte.	DAWES Jacob	M	-	Killed before Mooltan 6.11.48
2482	Pte.	DAY Isaac	M	G	Wounded before Mooltan 2.1.49
3230	Pte.	DELANEY Patrick	M	-	Discharged 13.8.50
670	Pte.	DEYKIN John	M	G	Discharged 13.8.50
3146	Pte.	DICKERSON John	M	-	Died 11.10.48
3084	Cpl.	DIXON Hugh	M	G	Wounded before Mooltan 12.9.48
2769	Pte.	DOGHERTY William	M	-	Wounded before Mooltan 12.9.48, discharged 23.10.49
1944	Pte.	DONALDSON Archibald	M	-	Wounded before Mooltan 6.11.48
753	Sjt.	DONNERY John	M	G	Died 20.11.50
1328	Pte.	DONAHUE Michael	M	G	Died 9.2.50
979	Pte.	DONOVAN Timothy	M	G	Wounded before Mooltan 6.11.48
2750	Pte.	DOOLIN Martin	M	G	Died 18.8.49
2882	Pte.	DOOLING John	Medal only		Died 21.8.48 en route to Mooltan
3231	Pte.	DOOLIN Patrick	M	G	Wounded before Mooltan 27.12.48
832	Pte.	DOONEY Peter	M	G	Discharged 10.9.50

1847	Cpl.	DOUGLAS George	M	-	Killed before Mooltan 12.9.48
2833	Pte.	DOWLING Thomas	M	G	Wounded before Mooltan 2.1.49
2583	Pte.	DOWLING William	M	G	Wounded in the City of Mooltan 9.1.49
3012	Pte.	DOWNES James	M	G	Drowned 6.12.50
3122	Pte.	DOYLE Thomas	M	G	Wounded at Goojerat 21.2.49
2783	Pte.	DUFFY Edward	M	G	Wounded before Mooltan 6.11.48
3160	Pte.	DULLARD Patrick	M	G	Discharged 21.10.50, permitted to reside in India
2279	Sjt.	DUNCOMBE James	M	G	Died 26.9.51
1379	Pte.	DUXIE John	M	G	Died 25.10.50
2973	Pte.	DWYER Patrick	M	G	Transferred to 53rd Foot 1.2.50
1943	Pte.	EGAN John	M	G	Wounded before Mooltan 10.9.48
3233	Pte.	EGANE John	M	-	Wounded before Mooltan 12.9.48
3175	Pte.	FALLON John	M	G	Wounded before Mooltan 6.11.48
3067	Pte.	FARRELL Thomas	Medal only		Died 22.5.51
3150	Pte.	FAULKNER James	M	G	Invalided 13.9.50, to England 1.2.51
2221	Pte.	FINCH James	M	-	Wounded before Mooltan 27.12.48, discharged 13.8.50
2327	Drummer.	FISHER Adolphus F.	Medal only		
2107	Pte.	FISHER William	M	G	Died 10.9.50
2537	Pte.	FLANAGAN John	M	G	Wounded before Mooltan 12.9.48
2214	Pte.	FLETCHER James	M	G	Died 2.7.49
2595	Pte.	FLINDERS Thomas	M	-	Died 15.10.50
1808	Pte.	FLYNN Patrick	M	G	Wounded before Mooltan 2.1.49
3046	Pte.	FLYNN Thomas	M	G	Wounded before Mooltan 29.12.48, discharged 10.9.50
2275	Sjt.	FORSYTH William	M	-	Killed before Mooltan 27.12.48
2702	Pte.	FOX William	M	G	Discharged 10.9.50
3156	Pte.	FRAWLEY Thomas	M	G	Wounded before Mooltan 12.9.48, discharged 23.10.49
2204	Pte.	FRIMLIN Thomas	Medal only		Died 21.8.48 en route to Mooltan
3168	Cpl.	GALLAGHER John	M	G	Died 4.1.52
2768	Pte.	GARAGHTY Richard	M	-	Killed before Mooltan 12.9.48
2637	Pte.	GATELY James	Medal only		
2839	Pte.	GEOGHEGAN Lawrence	M	G	Wounded at Goojerat 21.2.49
2434	Pte.	GILES William	M	-	Died of wounds 13.11.48
2444	Pte.	GILL Charles	M	G	Transfered to 3rd Lt.Dragoons 1.6.49
2988	Pte.	GLASS George	M	G	Wounded before Mooltan 2.1.49
1587	Pte.	GLENNON Cornelius	M	G	Discharged 10.9.50
2420	Pte.	GODBER John	M	G	Died 25.8.49
2402	Pte.	GOKESMITH William	M	G	Wounded before Mooltan 12.9.48
2324	Pte.	GOLDING George	M	-	Died 28.10.48
677	Pte.	GOODWIN Garnett	M	G	Invalided
3068	Pte.	GOTCHER John	M	-	Died of wounds 8.11.48, received 7.11.48
2085	Cpl.	GOUDY Edward K.	M	G	Wounded before Mooltan 12.9.48
987	Cpl.	GRAINGER George	M	G	Died 22.8.50
1026	Pte.	GRAINGER Henry	M	-	Killed before Mooltan 2.1.49
3069	Pte.	GREANEY Cornelius	M	G	Discharged 10.9.50
2423	Pte.	GRESHAM George H.	M	-	Died 3.1.49 from wounds received 2.1.49 at Mooltan

32nd Foot continued

2935	Pte.	GRIMES William	M	G	Free discharge 9.8.50
2185	Pte.	HALL John	M	G	Wounded before Mooltan 12.9.48
1848	Pte.	HAMILTON John	Medal only		
2475	Pte.	HANSON William	M	-	Killed before Mooltan 12.9.48
2706	Pte.	HARDING James	M	G	Died 24.10.49
1226	Pte.	HARDING William (1)	M	G	Drowned 10.5.50
3179	Pte.	HARFORD Samuel	M	-	Died 11.2.49
2745	Pte.	HARRIS John	M	G	Died 10.10.50
2509	Pte.	HARVEY George	M	-	Wounded before Mooltan 6.11.48
2398	Cpl.	HARVEY William	M	G	Discharge by purchase 1.10.49, to England.
2291	Sjt.	HATT William	M	-	Died of wounds 23.1.49, received at the storming of Mooltan 2.1.49
2962	Pte.	HAYDE Patrick	M	G	Wounded before Mooltan 12.9.48
1916	Pte.	HAYNES Thomas	M	G	Discharged 10.9.50
647	Sjt.	HENDERSON Michael	M	G	Discharged 13.8.50
2194	Pte.	HERD David	M	G	Discharge by purchase 1.8.49. Permitted to reside in India.
2992	Pte.	HICKEY William	M	-	Died 22.9.49
1011	Pte.	HILL William	M	G	Free discharge 9.8.50
2483	Pte.	HITCHCOCK Thomas	M	-	Wounded before Mooltan 12.9.48
2788	Pte.	HODGKIN George	M	-	Died 16.2.51
3048	Pte.	HODSON John	M	-	Died of Wounds 15.11.48 received 6.11.48
2827	Pte.	HORAN James	M	G	Wounded before Mooltan 12.9.48
2555	Cpl.	HOSE William	M	G	Invalided to England
2886	Pte.	HOURNEY Patrick	M	G	Wounded before Mooltan 2.1.49
2963	Pte.	HOWELLS Thomas	M	G	Free discharge 9.8.50
2964	Pte.	HUMPHREYS	M	G	Free discharge to England 1.2.51
2354	Pte.	HUNT Richard	M	G	Wounded before Mooltan 2.1.49, invalided 13.9.50, to England 1.2.51
2503	Pte.	JACKSON George	M	-	Died 26.11.48
	Lieut.	JEFFREY George	M	G	Wounded at Goojerat 21.2.49
2915	Pte.	JOHNSON Henry	M	-	Died of wounds 7.11.48, received 6.11.48
2650	Pte.	JOHNSON Nathaniel	M	G	Wounded before Mooltan 7.11.48
2824	Pte.	JONES Emanuel	M	G	Died 15.10.50
1896	Pte.	JONES Joseph	M	-	Died 22.2.49
2922	Cpl.	JONES Robert	M	G	Died 25.7.49
2815	Pte.	JONES Thomas (2)	Medal only		
1640	Pte.	JONES (1) William	M	G	Died 23.12.50
2778	Pte.	JOYCE James	M	-	Discharged 12.11.50
3253	Pte.	KAY Thomas	M	G	Died 12.8.50
3254	Pte.	KELLY John (2)	M	G	Wounded before Mooltan 2.1.49
3027	Pte.	KELLY Patrick	Medal only		
785	Pte.	KELSEY John	M	-	Invalided 13.9.50, to England 1.2.51
3255	Pte.	KENNEDY James	Medal only		Died 20.8.48
3128	Cpl.	KEOGH Denis	M	G	Discharged in India 2.9.51, enlisted in Bengal Artillery.
2559	Pte.	KEVINS Francis	M	G	Dead
1854	Sjt.	KIDNER David	M	G	Discharge by purchase 21.10.50, to England

	Capt.	KING Charles T.	M	G	Wounded before Mooltan 12.9.48 and 2.1.49
2940	Pte.	KINSELLA Patrick	M	G	Died 25.2.51
1661	Pte.	LAKIN Thomas	M	-	Died 6.5.49
2351	Pte.	LAVIS John	Medal only	Died 23.8.48 en route to Mooltan
2300	Pte.	LAW Edward	M	G	Died 22.8.50
2529	Pte.	LAWRENCE Irwin	Medal only	Died 22.8.49 en route to Mooltan
1347	Pte.	LEE William	M	-	Killed before Mooltan 6.11.48
2995	Pte.	LEECH Thomas	M	G	Discharged 8.1.50, to reside in India
2154	Pte.	LEWCAS George	Medal only	
1358	Pte.	LEY Samuel	M	-	Died 7.12.48
943	Pte.	LINFIELD William	M	G	Invalided 13.9.50, to England 1.2.51
665	Sjt.	LONNERGAN Thomas	M	G	Discharged 13.8.50
1933	Pte.	LUMBORD George	M	G	Wounded before Mooltan 12.9.48
3257	Pte.	LYONS Thomas	M	G	Died 30.4.50
2965	Pte.	McALISTER Henry	M	G	Invalided 15.9.50, to England 1.2.51
3026	Pte.	McALLISTER John	M	-	Wounded before Mooltan 12.9.48, discharged 25.10.49
2197	Pte.	McCURRY Archibald	M	G	Wounded at Mooltan 12.9.48
2890	Pte.	McDONOUGH Edward	M	-	Died of wounds 21.12.48 received 6.11.48
2743	Pte.	McDONOUGH Patrick	Medal only	
2807	Pte.	McGARRY James	M	G	Dead
726	Pte.	McGUIRE John	M	G	Free discharge to England 1.2.51
715	Cpl.	McGUIRE James	M	G	Wounded before Mooltan 2.1.49, discharged
3263	Pte.	McINTYRE Patrick	M	G	Wounded before Mooltan 12.9.48
3137	Pte.	McKENNA John	M	-	Died 19.11.48
2752	Pte.	McNABOUGH Francis	M	-	Died of wounds 3.1.49 received 27.12.48
3264	Pte.	McQUILLAN Owen	M	G	Died 13.2.51
3073	Pte.	MAHER Patrick	M	G	Died 10.11.49
2917	Pte.	MAHONEY Dennis	Medal only	
2963	Drummer.	MAHONEY John	Medal only	
3055	Pte.	MALLOY Peter	M	G	Died 27.8.50
1991	Pte.	MALTBY Joseph	M	-	Wounded before Mooltan 27.12.48
	Lt.Col.	MARKHAM Frederick C.B.	M	G	Wounded before Mooltan 10.9.48
1703	Pte.	MARLOW James	M	G	Free discharge to England 1.2.51
3053	Pte.	MARSHALL William	M	-	Invalided 28.8.50, to England 26.2.51
2113	Pte.	MATHER John	M	G	Wounded before Mooltan 27.12.48, discharged 13.8.50
1895	Pte.	MATTHEWS Thomas	M	G	Discharged by purchase 1.10.49, to England
	Lieut.	MAUNSELL Thomas	M	G	Wounded before Mooltan 21.1.49 to 28th Foot
2461	Pte.	MAYCOCK John	Medal only	
2641	Pte.	MELTON John	Medal only	Died 21.8.48 en route to Mooltan
1831	Pte.	MILLER Mark	M	G	Discharge by purchase 1.10.49, to England
1086	Clr.Sjt.	MITCHELL John	M	-	Died 9.11.48
1976	Drummer.	MOLLOY Francis	Medal only	Died 21.8.48 en route to Mooltan
2998	Pte.	MORRISSEY Joseph	M	-	Died 3.12.48
1537	Pte.	MORTIMORE Charles	Medal only	
2645	Pte.	MULRAY David	M	-	Wounded before Mooltan 12.9.48

32nd Foot continued

2770	Pte.	MURPHY William (1)	M	-	Died of wounds 19.11.48 received 6.11.48
3268	Pte.	MURPHY Thomas	M	-	Killed before Mooltan 6.11.48
1491	Drummer	MURRAY Daniel	M	G	Died 25.11.51
1937	Drummer	MURTAGH Nicholas	Medal only		Died 21.8.48 en route to Mooltan
1446	Pte.	NAPPER Thomas	M	G	Died 17.3.50
3269	Pte.	NARY John	M	G	Wounded before Mooltan 6.11.48
1220	Clr.Sjt.	NATTLE Peter	M	G	Committed suicide 26.4.49
2850	Pte.	NEILL James	M	G	Dead
1383	Pte.	NELSON Eli	M	G	Invalided 13.9.50, to England 1.2.51
1297	Pte.	NEWBURY George	M	G	Died 1.9.49
3270	Pte.	NIXON Jeffrey	M	G	Died 2.6.49
3001	Pte.	NOLAN Michael	M	-	Died 15.9.50
1315	Pte.	NORMAN Joseph	M	G	Wounded before Mooltan 12.9.48
1148	Drummer	NORMAN Thomas	Medal only		Died 3.4.49
3180	Pte.	O'BRIEN John	M	-	Wounded before Mooltan, discharged 23.10.50
2718	Pte.	O'BRIEN William	M	G ·	Discharged by purchase 21.10.50, to England
3271	Pte.	O'CONNOR Thomas	Medal only		
1559	Pte.	O'HARA James	M	G	Invalided 13.9.50, to England 1.2.51
3272	Pte.	O'KEEFFE George	M	G	Died 22.7.50
2721	Pte.	OUSLEY John	M	G	Wounded before Mooltan 27.12.48, discharged 24.9.50
1631	Pte.	PALMER William	M	G	Free discharge to England 1.2.51
1444	Pte.	PARR John	M	G	Died 31.10.50
1804	Pte.	PARSONS John (2)	M	G	Died 7.1.50
	Lt.Col.	PATTOUN Richard J.R.	M	-	Killed at Mooltan 12.9.48
3172	Pte.	PAYNE Philip	M	G	Invalided 13.9.50, to England 1.2.51
2329	Pte.	PEARCE James	M	G	Wounded before Mooltan 12.9.48
1159	Pte.	PEARCE William	Medal only		Died 11.8.48
3275	Pte.	PEARSON Charles	M	-	Died 3.1.49
3309	Pte.	PEARSON George (2)	M	-	Killed before Mooltan 2.1.49
2155	Pte.	PETTINGER Thomas	M	-	Killed before Mooltan 27.12.48
3276	Pte.	PHELAN Connor	M	-	Killed before Mooltan 2.1.49
1732	Pte.	PICKERING Joseph	M	-	Died 29.11.48
3076	Pte.	PINCHIM William	M	G	Invalided 13.9.50, to England 1.2.51
1890	· Pte.	PORTER James	M	G	Died 22.6.49
3187	Pte.	PORTER Thomas	M	G	Invalided 13.9.50, to England 1.2.51
3097	Pte.	PRESTON Joseph W.	M	G	Invalided 13.9.50, to England 1.2.51
2097	Cpl.	PURDUE Frederick	M	G	Wounded before Mooltan 6.11.48
3154	Pte.	PURTILL Thomas	M	G	Wounded before Mooltan 12.9.48
3181	Pte.	PURTILL William	M	-	Wounded before Mooltan 27.12.48, invalided 13.9.50, to England 1.2.51
3278	Pte.	RADFORD Leonard	M	-	Died 12.1.49
1620	Pte.	READY Patrick	M	G	Dead
2439	Pte.	REAISON Thomas	Medal only		
3002	Pte.	REED Patrick	M	-	Died 24.1.49
1252	Pte.	REYNOLDS Charles	M	G	Died 7.12.50
2087	Pte.	RICHMOND James	Medal only		
2766	Pte.	RIELLY George	M	G	Dead

2753	Pte.	ROBINSON James	Medal only		
3280	Pte.	ROCHE Richard	M	-	Died of wounds 13.9.48, received 12.9.48
1067	Pte.	ROURKE Michael (1)	M	-	Died of wounds 28.1.49, received 27.12.48
2886	Pte.	ROURKE Michael	M	G	Invalided 13.9.50, to England 1.2.51
3281	Pte.	ROUSE Richard	M	-	Killed before Mooltan 6.11.48
1900	Sjt.	ROWLAND John	M	G	Wounded before Mooltan 4.11.48
2072	Pte.	ROWSON John	M	-	Died 6.2.49
2491	Cpl.	RYDER John	M	G	Discharge by purchase 1.10.49, to England
1705	Pte.	SALTER William	M	G	Died 7.9.50
3059	Pte.	SAMMES Charles	M	-	Died 4.1.49
Medical Apprentice Subordinates		SCHANDLER John W.	M	G	Dismissed the service by sentence of a District Court Marshall
3283	Pte.	SCOTT Robert	M	-	Wounded before Mooltan 29.1.48, discharged 13.8.50
3284	Pte.	SCULLY James	M	G	Wounded before Mooltan 6.11.48
1292	Sjt.	SHAW William	M	G	Wounded before Mooltan 12.9.48
3286	Pte.	SHEAN Timothy	Medal only		Drowned in River Sutley 31.7.48
2948	Pte.	SHERIDAN Bartholomew	M	G	Wounded before Mooltan 27.12.48, invalided 13.9.50, to England 1.2.51
2207	Pte.	SHORT John	M	G	Died 5.1.51
1564	Sjt.	SLOANE Samuel	M	-	Died 14.5.51
2425	Pte.	SMALL Hugh	M	G	Died 14.10.49
2954	Clr.Sjt.	SMITH Alexander	M	G	Died 15.11.49
2634	Pte.	SMITH Henry	M	-	Died 16.1.49
1175	Pte.	SMITH James (1)	M	-	Died 19.6.49
3289	Pte.	SMITH John (4)	M	G	Died 27.5.49
3132	Pte.	SMITH Joseph	M	-	Wounded before Mooltan 12.9.48, discharged 13.8.50
2487	Sjt.	SMITH John	M	G	Died 26.3.51
3290	Pte.	SMITH Patrick	M	-	Wounded before Mooltan 27.12.48
	Capt.	SMYTH James D.C.	M	G	Wounded before Mooltan 2.1.49
983	Cpl.	SOLOMAN William	M	G	Died 5.5.49
1783	Pte.	SOMERVILLE David	M	G	Wounded before Mooltan 12.9.48
3092	Pte.	STANDLEY John	Medal only		Died 21.8.48 en route to Mooltan
1279	Pte.	STEVENS Reuben	M	G	Free discharge 9.8.50
1919	Sjt.	STEVENSON Robert	M	-	Died 4.11.48
	Lieut.	STEWART Houstoun	M	-	Died 2.9.49
1412	Pte.	STILES William	M	G	Free discharge 9.8.50
	Lieut.	STRAUBENZEE Bowen V.	M	-	Wounded before Mooltan 27.12.48
3294	Pte.	STREETS Thomas	M	-	Wounded before Mooltan 12.9.48, discharged 13.8.50
3295	Pte.	SUDDABY John	M	-	Discharged 10.9.50
687	Hosp.Sjt.	SULLIVAN John	M	G	Invalided 13.9.50, to England 1.2.51
3298	Pte.	SUNDERLAND Thomas	M	-	Died 24.6.49
	Lieut.	SWINBURNE John	M	G	Wounded before Mooltan 12.9.48, to 18th Foot
1541	Pte.	SYMONS Joseph	M	G	Died 5.4.49
2720	Pte.	TALLON Sylvester	M	G	Wounded before Mooltan 13.1.49
1500	Pte.	TAYLOR Edward	M	G	Died 9.3.49

	Qtr.Master	TAYLOR George	M	–	Died of wounds 12.9.48, received at Mooltan
3032	Pte.	TAYLOR James	Medal only		Died 21.8.48 en route to Mooltan
2357	Pte.	TAYLOR Richard	Medal only		
3299	Pte.	THOMPSON Robert (2)	M	–	Killed before Mooltan 12.9.48
3300	Pte.	THOMPSON William (2)	M	G	Wounded at Mooltan 27.12.48, discharged by purchase 21.10.50, to England
3301	Pte.	THOMPSON William (3)	Medal only		Died 12.8.48 en route to Mooltan
1430	Pte.	TILLEY Elijah	M	G	Wounded before Mooltan 12.9.48
2121	Pte.	TIMPSON Samuel	M	G	Wounded before Mooltan 12.9.48
2840	Pte.	TINDALE William	M	G	Wounded before Mooltan 27.12.48
1921	Pte.	TITTERTON John	M	G	Discharge by purchase 21.10.50 to England
2520	Pte.	TOFT John	M	–	Died 21.2.49
3302	Pte.	TOOLE Lawrence	M	G	Transfered to 24th Foot 1.10.50
3164	Pte.	TOWLE Thomas	Medal only		Died 21.8.48 en route to Mooltan
2259	Pte.	TROTER Thomas	M	G	Wounded before Mooltan 12.9.48
2569	Pte.	TULLY John	M	–	Died 6.12.48
3304	Pte.	TYLER William	Medal only		Died 21.8.48 en route to Mooltan
2642	Cpl.	VANCE James	M	G	Wounded before Mooltan 28.12.48
3305	Pte.	VERON Thomas	M	G	Wounded before Mooltan 12.9.48
1967	Pte.	VICKERS William	M	–	Wounded before Mooltan 2.1.49
3306	Pte.	WALL John	M	G	Wounded at Mooltan 2.1.49, died 1.1.51
2649	Pte.	WAPPLINGTON Mark	M	–	Died of wounds 13.9.48, received 12.9.48
515	Pte.	WARBURTON Henry	M	G	Died 26.2.50
3061	Pte.	WARBURTON James	M	G	Killed at Goojerat 21.2.49
2679	Pte.	WARD John	M	G	Wounded at Mooltan 2.1.49
1841	Pte.	WATKINS John	M	G	Wounded before Mooltan 12.9.48
2260	Cpl.	WATSON William	Medal only		Died 21.8.48 en route to Mooltan
	Capt.	WEARE Henry E.	M	–	To 50th Foot 15.8.48
2369	Pte.	WERE Richard	Medal only		Died 21.8.48 en route to Mooltan
1951	Pte.	WEST Elijah	M	G	Died 19.5.49
1953	Pte.	WHEATLEY Thomas	M	–	Died 17.12.50
2859	Pte.	WHELAN Thomas	M	G	Wounded at Goojerat 21.2.49
3007	Pte.	WHITE Martin	M	–	Died 13.11.48
2651	Pte.	WHITE Robert	M	G	Died 19.7.50
2953	Pte.	WHITEHEAD Thomas	M	G	Dead
1534	Pte.	WHITEHEAD William	M	G	Free discharge to England 1.2.51
2120	Pte.	WIDDOWSON William	M	–	Died 27.11.48
2504	Pte.	WIGHTAM William	M	G	Accidentally killed 22.7.49
3034	Pte.	WILLIAMS Charles	M	G	Died 10.10.49
1676	Cpl.	WILLIAMS Edwin	Medal only		
1462	Pte.	WILKINS John	M	G	Free discharge 9.9.50
1510	Pte.	WILLIAMSON Joseph	M	–	Invalided 13.9.50, to England 1.2.51
2451	Pte.	WILSON Matthew	M	G	Died 31.12.49
1499	Pte.	WITHERS John	M	G	Free discharge 8.4.51, to reside in India in private service of Col. Markham C.B.
2165	Pte.	WITT John	M	–	Killed at Mooltan 6.11.48
1475	Pte.	WOODLAND William	M	G	Free discharge 24.4.50 to England
1992	Pte.	WRIGHT Edwin	M	G	Wounded before Mooltan 27.12.48
633	Pte.	WRIGHTON John	M	G	Died 17.8.49

1742	Pte.	ASHWIN William	-	-	Died 24.7.49
1622	Drummer.	BARKER John	-	-	Died 18.12.48
1785	Pte.	BARNES Charles	-	G	Died 17.11.50
2780	Pte.	BARRY James	-	-	Died 5.1.49
2546	Pte.	BARTLETT Henry	-	-	Died 22.11.48
2496	Pte.	BARRETT Patrick	-	-	Died 24.10.48
1897	Cpl.	BAYHAM Frederick	-	G	To England 1.2.51
2967	Pte.	BIGGS Edward	-	-	Died 12.2.49
2317	Sjt.	BIRD Richard	-	-	Died 20.11.48
1898	Pte.	BREFFIT Nathaniel	-	G	Died 10.7.49
2778	Pte.	BROWN James	-	G	Died 20.6.49
1256	Pte.	BRYAN George	-	-	Died 16.11.48
2775	Pte.	BURKE Joseph	-	G	Died 8.4.49
730	Pte.	BURKE Patrick	-	G	Died 29.11.49
2554	Pte.	CAMPBELL William	-	-	Died 6.7.49
1937	Pte.	CALLWELL William	-	G	Died 12.11.49
2142	Pte.	CANDLISH Charles	-	G	Died 6.6.49
2033	Pte.	CANE Patrick	-	-	Died 5.2.49
1780	Pte.	CASEY James	-	G	Died 17.10.49
2415	Pte.	CHERRY John	-	-	Died 11.11.49
2690	Pte.	CLAYTON Thomas	-	-	Died 5.11.49
2784	Pte.	COLLER Jeremiah	-	G	Died 4.8.49
1985	Pte.	CONNELL Andrew	-	-	Died 26.11.48
2194	Pte.	CONNOR Michael	-	-	Died 11.11.48
2782	Pte.	CONNOR Sylvester	-	-	Died 6.12.48
2658	Pte.	CONWAY Thomas	-	G	Died 6.1.51
1987	Pte.	CUNNINGHAM Peter	-	G	Died 28.12.49
2508	Pte.	CURRANE Daniel	-	-	Died 29.9.49
2566	Pte.	DANIELS Isaac	-	G	Died 18.7.49
1121	Pte.	DAVIES Richard	-	-	Died 20.12.48
888	Cpl.	DAY George	-	G	Died 3.10.49
2253	Pte.	DEERY Thomas	-	G	Died 27.2.49
887	Pte.	DUTTON Samuel	-	G	Died 18.6.49
2706	Pte.	EARLE John	-	-	Died 30.3.49
2796	Pte.	EDWARDS John	-	-	Died 26.1.50
1563	Cpl.	EFFINGHAM John	-	G	Died 25.8.49
2511	Pte.	ERSKINE William	-	G	Discharge by purchase 16.5.50
2436	Pte.	EVANS Joseph	-	G	Died 26.1.50
1503	Sjt.	EVERARD Peter	-	-	Died 10.5.49
2648	Pte.	FALLEN Thomas	-	G	Died 11.6.49
2159	Pte.	FINN William	-	-	Died 20.10.48
2538	Pte.	FITZGERALD John	-	-	Died 27.5.49
2513	Pte.	FORD Thomas	-	G	Died 8.5.49
1992	Pte.	FOY John	-	-	Died 9.11.48
2514	Pte.	FUORHAN John	-	-	Died 24.9.49
1476	Pte.	GLANVILLE George	-	-	Died 17.5.49

53rd Foot continued

1869	Pte.	GOODALL William	·	·	Died 5.2.50
2695	Pte.	GOMERSON James	·	G	Died 2.11.49
2790	Pte.	GORMAN Michael	-	-	Died 17.10.49
2441	Pte.	GREEN Matthew	-	G	Died 23.2.50
2788	Pte.	GRIFFIN James	-	-	Died 22.10.49
2697	Pte.	GRIFFITHS John	-	-	Died 24.6.49
1695	Pte.	GROWCOTT Stephen	-	-	Died 21.12.48
2140	Pte.	HALLY Charles	-	-	Died 23.12.50
2039	Pte.	HANNON Patrick	-	-	Died 12.7.50
2239	Pte.	HARDESTY Richard	-	G	Died 23.12.50
2677	Pte.	HARRISON George	-	G	Died 23.9.49
1996	Pte.	HEALY Dennis	-	-	Died 9.11.48
1462	Pte.	HOCKIN William	-	G	Died 25.11.50
2080	Pte.	HOGAN Timothy	-	-	Died 7.7.50
1224	Cpl.	HOLLAND William	-	-	Died 14.1.49
2041	Pte.	HOLMES John	-	G ·	Discharge by purchase 21.9.49
2440	Pte.	HOLT Abraham	-	-	Died 14.1.49
2582	Pte.	HOWARD Patrick	-	-	Died 16.5.49
1875	Pte.	INGRAM William	-	C	Died 30.6.49
1566	Pte.	JOHNSON James	-	-	Died 10.12.49
2453	Pte.	JONES Samuel	-	G	Died 8.6.51
2805	Pte.	KELIHER Michael	-	-	Died 11.12.48
1818	Pte.	KENNEDY Charles	-	G	Deserted 11.7.49
2227	Pte.	KING George	-	G	Died 18.2.50
2589	Pte.	KING Samuel	-	G	Discharge by purchase 11.1.50 Died before Lepuinghq.
2534	Clr.Sjt.	LOCKE Henry	-	G	Discharge 24.8.49, re-enlisted 25.3.51
1669	Pte.	LOGAN ALEXANDER	-	-	Died 24.5.49
2760	Pte.	LONG Joseph	-	G	Died 15.4.50
2724	Pte.	LOVELL Thomas G.	-	-	Died 30.9.50
2751	Pte.	LOVICK Robert	-	G	Died 18.12.49
1604	Pte.	LUCAS John	-	G	Died 2.8.49
2819	Pte.	LUDDY John	-	-	Died 19.10.50
1880	Pte.	McDERMOTT Cornelius	-	G	Died 27.8.49
2826	· Pte.	McGAWLEY Thomas	-	-	Died 20.1.49
2157	Pte.	McKAY John	-	G	Died 4.6.49
1702	ORC	McKAY G.D.	-	G	Discharge by purchase 21.7.49
979	Sjt.	McKEE Richard	-	-	Died 10.7.50
1804	Pte.	McNALLY George	-	-	Died 21.11.49
2171	Pte.	MAGEE William	-	-	Recommended to be discharged with ignomy
2817	Pte.	MAHONEY Michael	-	-	Died 29.12.48
2030	Pte.	MACKIMSON William	-	-	Discharge by purchase 8.11.49
2596	Pte.	MAY Laurence	-	G	Died 23.6.50
1914	Pte.	MEEHAN Cornelius	-	G	Died 28.12.49
2520	Pte.	MERIDITH Evan	-	-	Died 10.12.48
1540	Pte.	MONK George	-	-	Died 28.11.49
2522	Pte.	MOORE Paul	-	·	Died 3.7.50

2151	Pte.	MORRISON Matthew	-	-	Died 27.11.48
2062	Pte.	MULCAHI Martholomew	-	G	Discharge by purchase 23.9.50
2271	Pte.	MULLIGAN James	-	G	Died 16.12.49
2131	Pte.	MULRY John	-	G	Died 13.8.49
1881	Pte.	MURPHY Michael	-	-	Transfered to 70th Foot 1.4.51
1721	Clr.Sjt.	NADIN Miles	-	G	Died 25.3.50
1621	Drummer	NEWLANDS Alexander	-	-	Embarked 7.4.51 for discharge with igmoniny
1736	Pte.	NORMAN William	-	G	Died 20.11.49
1681	Pte.	PARKER Joseph	-	G	Died 15.7.49
1732	Pte.	PARSONS Philip	-	G	Died 20.2.50
2540	Cpl.	PEARCE Thomas	-	G	Died 21.10.49
1799	Pte.	PERRY Alexander	-	-	Died 25.9.49
1543	Pte.	PIERCE Edward	-	-	Died 23.9.49
948	Pte.	PIERCE Joseph	-	-	Died 18.11.48
1885	Pte.	PROCTOR Matthew	-	-	Died 15.10.48
2860	Pte.	PULLEN George	-	-	Died 16.10.48
2535	Sjt.	REED James	-	G	Free discharge 18.10.49
1795	Pte.	REID Bernard	-	-	Died 28.10.48
1236	Drum Major	REYNOLDS Johns	-	-	Died 30.9.49
2831	Pte.	ROACH William	-	-	Discharged by purchase 4.9.50, died en route to Bombay
2859	Pte.	ROACH William	-	G	Died 9.2.50
2134	Pte.	RODDEN Francis	-	-	Died 9.12.48
2184	Pte.	ROE John	-	G	Died 4.7.49
2354	Pte.	SAVELE William	-	-	Died 6.11.50
1823	Pte.	SHARPS William	-	G	Died 6.4.50
788	Pte.	SMALLWOOD George	-	G	Died 9.10.50
2213	Pte.	SMITH James	-	-	Died 10.7.49
2051	Pte.	SMITH Rowland	-	G	Died 20.12.49
2020	Pte.	SMITH Thomas	-	-	Died 27.12.48
1820	Sch.Mst.Sjt.	STEWART Robert H.	-	-	Died 9.12.49
2618	Pte.	STRANGE John	-	G	Died 20.5.50
2620	Pte.	SUTTON James	-	G	Died 31.12.49
2527	Pte.	THOMAS John	-	-	Executed for murder 15.2.49
2180	Pte.	TOTTEN William	-	G	Died 24.10.49
2484	Pte.	TRAYNOR Patrick	-	G	Died 2.10.49
1931	Pte.	TUCKER William	-	G	Died 28.6.49
1782	Pte.	UPSHALL Charles	-	-	To 22nd Foot 1.5.50
2235	Pte.	VAIL Patrick	-	-	Died 13.5.49
974	Pte.	VINEY Shadrack	-	G	Died 26.7.49
	Lieut.	WADDILOVE F.W.D.	-	-	Died 4.6.49
2023	Pte.	WALLACE John	-	-	Died 27.8.49
2116	Pte.	WARES John	-	G	Died 5.7.49
2276	Pte.	WATLEY James	-	-	Died 11.12.49
2117	Pte.	WILLCOTT Samuel	-	-	Died 31.12.48
1746	Pte.	WILLIAMS Thomas	-	G	Died 11.8.50
2390	Pte.	WILLIS John	-	G	To 70th Foot 1.5.51

| 985 | Pte. | WOODALL John | - | - | Died 3.8.49 |
| 2058 | Pte. | WYATT Henry | - | G | Deserted 11.7.49 |

* * *

1/60th FOOT

2345	Pte.	ADAMS Charles	M	-	Discharged by purchase 31.8.50
2506	Pte.	ADDY John	M	G	Invalided 24.9.50, to England 23.2.51
1656	Pte.	ALEXANDER John	M	G	Died 31.7.49
2111	Pte.	ALLEN Charles	M	-	Wounded at Mooltan
2556	Pte.	ALLEN John	M	G	Died 19.6.49
2587	Pte.	ALLT William	M	-	Wounded at Mooltan
880	Pte.	ANDREWS Edwin	M	G	Died 15.11.50
1727	Pte.	ANNAND James	M	G	Died
2218	Pte.	ANTCLIFFE Robert	M	G	Discharged by purchase 9.3.50
1820	Pte.	ARMINGER Christopher	M	G	Died 13.8.49
1809	Pte.	ARMISTEAD William	M	-	Invalided 1.11.49, to England 26.1.50
1645	Pte.	ATKINSON John	M	G	Wounded at Mooltan
1064	Pte.	AYLESBURY Henry	M	-	Killed 21.1.49
2509	Pte.	BARTLETT James	M	G	Invalided 17.9.49, to England 1.3.50
914	Pte.	BARTLETT William	M	G	Invalided 24.9.50, to England 23.2.51
2568	Pte.	BARWELL Edward	M	G	Died 3.3.49
2638	Pte.	BEARDSLEY Joseph	M	-	Died 21.1.49
1277	Pte.	BEGGS Michael	M	G	Invalided 17.9.49, to England 1.3.50
2373	Pte.	BETTS William	M	G	Invalided 24.9.50, to England 23.2.51
2219	Pte.	BIGGS Joseph	M	G	Discharged by purchase 2.2.50
1050	Sjt.	BISHOP James	M	G	Invalided 17.9.49, to England 1.3.50
1863	Pte.	BLAIR James	M	-	Invalided 30.10.49, to England 26.1.50
2132	Pte.	BOND Henry	M	G	Died
2492	Pte.	BOOTH John	M	-	Died 4.6.51
2072	Pte.	BOWDEN George	M	G	Died 19.6.49
1487	Pte.	BOWSHER James	M	G	Discharged by purchase 31.8.50
2359	Pte.	BRACEY John	M	G	Invalided 24.9.50, to England 23.2.51
1369	Cpl.	BRENNAN James	M	G	Discharged by purchase 18.8.50
	2/Lt.	BROOKE Robert H.	M	G	Wounded at Mooltan
2042	Pte.	BROWN John (1st)	M	G	Discharged by purchase 15.2.50
1960	Cpl.	BROWN Thomas (1st)	M	G	Died 19.7.49
2025	Pte.	BRUCE Robert	M	G	Died 5.12.49
1285	Pte.	BRYAN James (1st)	M	G	Invalided 24.9.50, to England 23.2.51
2460	Pte.	BRYCE John	M	G	Invalided 24.9.50, to England 23.2.51
2542	Pte.	BURKE James	M	G	Died
180	Pte.	BURNS Thomas	M	-	Invalided 17.9.49, permitted to remain in India
2310	Cpl.	BURTON Joseph	M	G	Died 15.4.51
2593	Pte.	BUTCHER Isaac	M	G	Invalided 24.9.50, to England 23.2.51
2594	Pte.	BUTCHER Moses	M	-	Invalided 24.9.50, to England 23.2.51
2224	Pte.	CAIN John	M	-	Invalided 30.10.49, to England 26.1.50
2654	Pte.	CALVERT John Ferdinand	M	G	Died 19.7.49
709	Sjt.	CAMERON Alexander	M	G	Invalided 24.9.50, to England 23.2.51

2251	Pte.	CARRIGG William John	M	G	Discharge by purchase 28.3.50
2596	Pte.	CARTER George	M	-	Killed 28.12.48
2541	Bugler	CAWDRON Robert	M	-	Wounded at Mooltan
1493	Pte.	CHALLIS John	M	G	Discharge by purchase 31.8.50
2328	Pte.	CHAPMAN Joseph	M	G	Died 26.6.49
1467	Cpl.	CHIPP John	M	G	Discharge by purchase 7.9.50
2653	Pte.	CHOLEMAN John	M	G	Invalided 24.9.50 to England 23.2.51
2657	Pte.	CLARKE George (2)	M	-	Killed 27.12.48
1961	Pte.	CLEMENTS William	M	G	Discharged 20.8.51
2074	Pte.	COLLINS Lot	M	G	Invalided 24.9.50 to England 23.2.51
2394	Bugler	COLLINS James	M	G	Wounded at Goojerat
2075	Pte.	CONDON Michael	M.	G	Invalided 24.9.50 to England 23.2.51
2659	Pte.	CONNELL John	M	G	Killed in action 14.12.49
620	Q.Mst.Sjt.	COOK John	M	-	Accidentaly drowned at Mooltan 30.12.48
2009	Pte.	COSTELLO James	M	G	Invalided 17.9.49 to England 1.1.50 Died at Sea
2116	Pte.	COUCHMAN Amos	M	G	Died 20.11.50
845	Pte.	COULTER James	M	G	Died 26.11.49
1791	Pte.	COWIE William	M	-	Wounded at Mooltan died 15.2.50
2253	Cpl.	COX Levi	M	G	Discharge by purchase 29.10.50
2383	Pte.	CRAWFORD Richard	M	G	Discharge by purchase 31.12.49
895	Pte.	CREYS Thomas	M	-	Died 10.6.49
2076	Pte.	CROSS John	M	G	Invalided 24.9.50 to England 23.2.51
1750	Pte.	CULLEN John (1st)	M	G	Invalided 24.9.50 to England 23.2.51
2598	Pte.	CUSACK James	M	-	Wounded at Mooltan, invalided 30.10.49, to England 26.1.50
827	Pte.	DAGG William	M	G	Died 20.12.50
2431	Cpl.	DALTON William	M	G	Died 20.11.49
2669	Pte.	DAVIN Patrick	M	G	Died 4.12.49
777	Sjt.	DAVIS Hugh	M	G	Invalided 24.9.50, to England 23.2.51
2672	Pte.	DAVIS Michael	M	G	Transferred 22nd Foot 31.5.51, to serve with an elder brother
2580	Pte.	DELAHUNTY Martin	M	-	Killed 21.1.49
	Major	DENNIS Maurice	M	G	Wounded at Mooltan
2666	Pte.	DENNY John	M	G	Died 13.7.49
1981	Pte.	DILLON Patrick	M	G	Invalided 17.9.49, to England 1.3.50
2512	Pte.	DOYLE Charles	M	-	Invalided 24.9.50, to England 23.2.51
2549	Pte.	DUFFIN Samuel	M	G	Transfered 14th Lt.Dgns 1.10.49, to serve with an elder brother
1341	Pte.	DWYER Anthony	M	G	Transferred 22nd Foot 31.12.50 to serve with an elder brother
1523	Pte.	EADY James	M	G	Died 20.6.49
791	Clr.Sjt.	EAGAR William	M	G	Invalided 24.9.50, to England 23.2.51
1939	Sch.Mst.Sjt.	EDINGTON William	M	-	Discharge by purchase 9.12.50
2680	Pte.	EDMOND Alexander	M	G	Invalided 17.9.49, to England 1.3.50
2465	Pte.	ESSON Robert	M	-	Wounded at Mooltan, invalided 30.10.49, to England 26.1.50
2228	Cpl.	FARMER William	M	G	Discharge by purchase 31.12.49
1284	Pte.	FARRACY Patrick	M	G	Died 2.5.51
2364	Pte.	FINDER William	M	G	Invalided 17.9.49 to England 1.3.50

1/60th Foot continued

1600	Pte.	FITCH Richard	M	G	Discharge by purchase 8.2.51
1959	Pte.	FITZPATRICK Matthias M.	M	G	Died 27.10.49
2683	Pte.	FLYNN Patrick	M	G	Died 18.11.49
934	Bugle Major	FOGHILL Charles	M	G	Free discharge 28.2.50
242	Clr.Sjt.	FORBES John	M	G	Invalided 17.9.49, to England 1.3.50
2121	Cpl.	FULLER Richard	M	G	Died
2229	Pte.	GAWLEY William	M	-	Invalided 30.10.49, to England 26.1.50
1165	Pte.	GEDLING Thomas	M	G	Invalided 17.9.49, to England 1.3.50
2515	Pte.	GEEVES John	M	-	Invalided 30.10.49, to England 26.1.50
762	Pte.	GEORGE William	M	G	Invalided 24.9.50, to England 23.2.51
2348	Pte.	GILLIGAN Michael	M	G	Died 23.2.49
1929	Sjt.	GODKIN Joseph	M	G	Discharge by purchase 28.3.50
1671	Pte.	GOODHALL George Aaron	M	-	Invalided 24.9.50, to England 23.2.51
2158	Pte.	GOODY John	M	G	Discharge by purchase 7.9.50
	Major	GORDON John	M	-	Killed at Mooltan 27.12.48
2687	Pte.	GRACE Edward	M	G	Died 13.8.49
2321	Pte.	GULLIVER Peter	M	-	Killed 27.12.48
2983	Pte.	HAMMOND Robert	M	G	Died 23.12.49
1801	Sjt.	HARGREAVES James	M	G	Discharge by purchase 28.3.50
1552	Pte.	HARRIS Edmund	M	G	Discharge by purchase 21.9.50
2139	Pte.	HARRIS John	M	G	Died 2.6.51
2692	Pte.	HAWKINS George	M	G	Died
1379	Pte.	HAYDON William	M	G	Died 23.8.50
2138	Pte.	HEAVER Edward	M	G	Wounded at Mooltan
2693	Pte.	HENNESSY David	M	-	Died 3.12.49
2279	Pte.	HENSON Thomas	M	G	Died 31.3.49
868	Cpl.	HEWITT John	M	G	Invalided 24.9.50, to England 23.2.51
2365	Pte.	HILL Benjamin	M	G	Invalided 24.9.50 to England 23.2.51
2350	Pte.	HILL John	M	-	Wounded at Mooltan, invalided 1.11.49, to England 26.1.50
2604	Pte.	HILL Matthew	M	G	Free discharge 28.3.50
452	S/Major	HINDLE Edwin	M	-	Invalided 17.9.49, to England 26.1.50
2018	Pte.	HODGSON Thomas	M	G	Died 12.11.50
2178	Pte.	HOOPER John	M	G	Died 8.7.50
2608	Pte.	HORNSBY Samuel	M	G	Invalided 24.9.50, to England 23.2.51
1186	Pte.	HOSCROFT Samuel	M	-	Died
1714	Pte.	HOWARD John	M	G	Invalided 24.9.50, to England 23.2.51
2081	Pte.	HULES James	M	G	Discharge by purchase 28.9.50
2082	Pte.	HULSE William	M	G	Died 23.12.19
1470	Pte.	HUMPHRIES James (1st)	M	-	Died 8.4.49
1736	Pte.	HUNTER Thomas (1st)	M	G	Died 3.2.51
2480	Pte.	HUNTER Thomas (2nd)	M	-	Died 28.7.49
2085	Pte.	HUSSEY William	M	G	Discharge by purchase 31.8.50
1648	Pte.	HUTCHISON James	M	G	Discharged
1841	Pte.	HUTTON William	M	G	Discharged by purchase 2.2.50
1589	Pte.	HYDE Isaac	M	G	Died 10.5.51
2128	Pte.	JACKSON George	M	G	Discharged by purchase 31.12.49
2355	Pte.	JAMES Joseph	M	G	Wounded at Mooltan

1689	Pte.	JENKISSON John	M	G	Invalided 24.9.50, to England 23.2.51
710	Pte.	JOSS James	M	G	Invalided 24.9.50, to England 23.2.51
2701	Pte.	JOYCE Thomas	M	-	Wounded at Mooltan
2181	Pte.	KEARNEY Thomas	M	G	Invalided 24.9.50, to England 23.2.51
946	Pte.	KEMP David	M	G	Invalided 17.9.49, to England 1.3.50
1564	Pte.	KENTY John	M	G	Discharge by purchase 5.2.51
1901	Pte.	KENYON John	M	G	Died 31.3.51
1043	Pte.	KITCHEN William	M	G	Died
254	Q.M.Sjt.	KITTLES George	M	G	Invalided 24.9.50, to England 23.2.51
2711	Pte.	LANGLEY John	M	-	Wounded at Mooltan
2210	Pte.	LAMBERT John	M	G	Invalided 24.9.50, to England 23.2.51
2473	Pte.	LAYCOCK John	M	G	Died 31.12.50
2298	Pte.	LEAHY William	M	G	Died 18.5.51
1246	Pte.	LEE George	M	-	Wounded at Mooltan to 22nd Foot 28.2.51 to serve with an older brother
714	Sjt.	LEE William	M	G	Invalided 24.9.50, to England 23.2.51
2534	Pte.	LEGGETT James	M	G	Wounded at Mooltan
1948	Pte.	LLOYD Benjamin	M	G	Died 21.4.49
2237	Pte.	LOVE George	M	G	Died 16.9.50
1289	Pte.	LOWERY James	M	G	Died 29.10.49
246	Pte.	LUDFORD James	M	G	Invalided 17.9.49, to England 1.3.50
1343	Pte.	LYONS Michael	M	G	Invalided 24.9.50, to England 23.2.51
2474	Pte.	McARTHUR Peter	M	G	Discharge by purchase 28.3.50
2339	Pte.	McCAULEY Robert	M	-	Invalided 1.11.49, to England 26.1.50
684	Pte.	McCULLEN Patrick	M	G	Invalided 17.9.49, permitted to remain in India
2717	Pte.	McDONOGH Bartholomew	M	G	Died 10.10.49
2616	Pte.	McDONOGH Robert	M	G	Died 7.7.50
1354	Pte.	McEVENEY George	M	G	Died 9.5.51
151	Pte.	McKAY Murdock	M	G	Died 8.3.49
1953	Pte.	McKAY Robert	M	G	Discharge by purchase 25.10.50, wounded at Mooltan
1248	Pte.	McKINNON Angus	M	G	Free discharge 10.3.51
2260	Pte.	McROBBIE David	M	G	Discharge by purchase 9.3.50
1114	Pte.	MAIN John	M	G	Died 3.8.50
1669	Pte.	MARSHALL Joshua	M	G	Discharge by purchase 31.8.50
2153	Pte.	MASKALL William Henry	M	G	Died
877	Pte.	MAYLARD George	M	G	Invalided 24.9.50, to England 23.2.51
2208	Pte.	MEEK James	M	G	Discharg by purchase 28.3.50
1128	Pte.	MIDGLEY Robert	M	G	Discharge by purchase 31.10.50, since enlisted 22nd Foot.
2611	Pte.	MILLS John	M	-	Wounded at Mooltan
1194	Sjt.	MILLS William	M	G	Invalided 24.9.50, to England 23.2.51
2406	Pte.	MITCHELL Richard	M	G	Died 26.12.49
2478	Pte.	MOORE John	M	G	Discharge by purchase 9.3.50
2553	Pte.	MORGAN Thomas	M	G	Died 13.6.49
245	Clr.Sjt.	MULLIGAN James	M	G	Invalided 17.9.49, to England 1.3.50
2726	Pte.	MURPHY Patrick	M	G	Died 28.1.50
1690	Pte.	MURRAY Alexander	M	G	Invalided 17.9.49, to England 1.3.50

1328	Pte.	MURRAY James	M	G	Killed in action 14.12.49
737	Pte.	NEEN Isaac	M	G	Invalided 17.9.49, to England 1.3.50
2060	Pte.	NEWTON Robert	M	G	Discharge by purchase 7.9.50
1919	Sjt.	NICHOLSON Samuel	M	-	Discharge by purchase 28.11.50
2092	Pte.	NOLAN William	M	G	Deserted 4.4.51
2613	Pte.	NUTTER William	M	-	Wounded at Mooltan
2729	Pte.	OAKLEY Walter	M	-	Invalided 1.11.49, to England 26.1.50
1296	Pte.	O'BRIEN Charles	M	G	Died 19.9.49
2614	Pte.	O'CONNELL James	M	G	Transferred to 22nd Foot 31.12.50, to serve with elder brother
734	Pte.	O'KEEFE Michael	M	G	Invalided 24.9.50, to England 23.2.51
2731	Pte.	O'NEILL Daniel	M	G	Died 13.8.49
2147	Pte.	OWEN John	M	G	Discharge by purchase 7.2.50
701	Pte.	OWENS Henry	M	G	Invalided 24.9.50, to England 23.2.51
1452	Pte.	PAINE George	M	G	Died 25.12.50
1623	Pte.	PARKER Richard	M	G	Died 1.3.51
1997	Pte.	PARKINSON William	M	G	Died
1970	Pte.	PARRY Richard	M	G	Free discharge to England 23.2.51
2330	Pte.	PICKARD David	M	G	Died 31.10.49
2761	Pte.	PITTARD Walter	M	G	Died 7.7.49
2352	Pte.	PITTS James	M	G	Died 3.8.50
2736	Pte.	PLATT Jacob	M	G	Died 6.8.49
2149	Pte.	PORTER George	M	-	Killed 28.12.48
1918	Cpl.	POWER James	M	G	Discharge by purchase 30.1.50
1962	Sjt.	PRITCHARD George Munn	M	G	Died 11.4.51
1604	Sjt.	PUGH William	M	G	Invalided 17.9.49, to England 1.3.50
1157	Pte.	QUINN John William	M	-	Wounded at Mooltan
1258	Pte.	QUIRK Richard	M	G	Died 31.1.51
2742	Pte.	RAE James	M	G	Discharge by purchase 25.10.50
2424	Pte.	RAMSAY William	M	G	Died 24.3.50
2743	Pte.	READ Samuel	M	G	Died 4.8.49
2744	Pte.	REARDON Michael	M	-	Wounded at Mooltan, invalided 1.11.49, to England 26.1.50
1976	Pte.	REDDY Alfred	M	G	Transferred 3rd Lt.Dgns to serve with elder brother 1.10.49
814	Pte.	REILLY John	M	G	Invalided 24.9.50, to England 23.2.51
2745	Pte.	REILLY John	M	G	Died 12.8.49
2296	Pte.	RILEY Henry	M	G	Died 15.12.50
2188	Sjt.	ROBINSON John	M	G	Invalided 24.9.50, to England 23.2.51
1824	Pte.	ROILEY John	M	-	Wounded at Mooltan
2752	Pte.	SALT George	M	G	Died 7.11.49
1631	Sjt.	SANSOM James	M	G	Died 24.6.49
1197	Pte.	SCOTT James	M	G	Discharge by purchase 30.1.50
722	Pte.	SCOTT Thomas	M	G	Invalided 24.9.50, to England 23.2.51
1568	Pte.	SHAW Nicholas	M	G	Invalided 17.9.49, to England 1.3.50
1162	Pte.	SIMPSON Thomas	M	G	Died 29.12.50
2758	Pte.	SLATTERY James	M	G	Died
1893	Pte.	SLOMAN Henry	M	G	Died 27.2.49

1520	Pte.	SMITH George (1st)	M	G	Invalided 24.9.50, to England 23.2.51
1094	Pte.	SMITH John (1st)	M	G	Died 8.7.49
2619	Pte.	SMITH John (3rd)	M	-	Killed at Mooltan
2620	Pte.	SMITH William (2nd)	M	G	Invalided 24.9.50, to England 23.2.51
1646	Pte.	SNELL James	M	G	Discharged by purchase 26.4.50
680	Pte.	SPLAHAN John	M	-	Invalided 17.9.49, to England 26.1.50
2100	Pte.	STEPHENSON Andrew	M	G	Died 5.1.51
2763	Pte.	SULLIVAN Bartholomew	M	-	Killed 29.12.48
1262	Sjt.	SUTTON John	M	G	Died 13.4.51
2583	Pte.	SWITZER James	M	G	To 96th Foot 31.1.50, to serve with elder brother
2422	Bugler	TAYLOR William	M	G	Discharged by purchase 9.3.50
1765	Sjt.	THEOBALD Charles	M	-	Killed 20.1.49
1129	Pte.	THORPE John	M	G	Invalided 17.9.49, to England 1.3.50
2770	Pte.	UPTON Luke	M	G	Died 12.8.49
1612	Pte.	VENVELL William	M	G	Discharged by purchase 8.2.51
2622	Pte.	WALEY Thomas	M	-	Invalided 24.9.50, to England 23.2.51. Confined prisoner 16.1.49, tried by General Court Marshall 24.5.49 - Aquitted.
2773	Pte.	WALKER William (2nd)	M	G	Discharge by purchase 2.12.49
255	Bugler	WALSH James (1st)	M	G	Invalided 24.9.50, to England 23.2.51
1148	Pte.	WALSH Joseph	M	G	Free discharge 28.3.50
1471	Pte.	WALSH William (1st)	M	G	Discharged by purchase 28.3.50
2439	Pte.	WALSH William (2nd)	M	G	Discharged
1324	Pte.	WARD John	M	G	Invalided 24.9.50, to England 23.2.51
2779	Pte.	WARNER Robert	M	G	Died 28.7.49
423	Pte.	WARRINGTON John	M	G	Invalided 17.9.49, to England 1.3.50
2107	Pte.	WATT Thomas	M	-	Killed 18.1.49
859	Pte.	WEBB William	M	G	Invalided 24.9.50, to England 23.2.51
1829	Pte.	WELLS George	M	G	Wounded at Mooltan
1811	Pte.	WHITE Edward	M	G	Died 11.8.49
2420	Pte.	WHITE Robert	M	G	Died 21.6.49
2780	Pte.	WHITE William	M	-	Wounded at Mooltan
1748	Pte.	WHITEHEAD Stanoth	M	G	Died 23.7.50
2392	Pte.	WILLIAMS John	M	-	Died 31.1.49
1193	Pte.	WILSON Thomas	M	G	To England - free discharge 23.2.51
1720	Pte.	WOOD James (1st)	M	G	Discharged
2154	Pte.	WOOD Matthew	M	G	Died 22.9.49
2163	Pte.	WRIGHT William	M	G	Died 6.11.49
2276	Pte.	YOUART James	M	G	Invalided 17.9.49, to England 1.3.50, Retired India 28.6.51

* * *

61st FOOT

855	Cpl.	ALLEN Ellis	Medal only		Died 25.7.49
2618	Pte.	ANDERSON David	C	G	Died 24.4.51
1774	Pte.	ANDREW Ralph	C	G	Died 21.10.50
	Lieut.	ARMSTRONG Archibald	C	G	Died 24.10.50

1679	Cpl.	ASHTON Samuel	C	G	Died 10.6.50
1007	Clr.Sjt.	AXION Martin	C	G	Died 7.5.51
2235	Pte.	BAKER David	C	G	Wounded at Chilianwala
2535	Pte.	BARLOW Joseph	C	G	Wounded at Chilianwala
1406	Sjt.	BARNETT James	C	G	Wounded at Sadoolopore
2143	Pte.	BARRETT James	C	G	Died of Wounds 22.2.49 received at Goojerat
1986	Pte.	BAXTER Francis	C	G	Died 18.7.50
2201	Pte.	BAYES John	C	G	Died 9.5.50
1625	Pte.	BEECROFT John	C	G	Wounded at Chilianwala
1450	Pte.	BELL John	C	G	Wounded at Chilianwala
583	Pte.	BERFORD James	C	G	Wounded at Chilianwala
2161	Sjt.	BINGLEY George	C	G	Died 4.12.49
585	Pte.	BLAGG James	C	G	Died 28.4.49
1209	Pte.	BLAKE Patrick	C	G	Died 29.6.49
2543	Pte.	BLIZZARD Thomas	C	G	Free discharge 15.2.50
757	Pte.	BOGGS James	C	G	Wounded at Chilianwala
1129	Cpl.	BOWEN Michael	C	G	Wounded at Chilianwala
1080	Pte.	BOYLE James	C	G	Wounded at Goojerat
2241	Pte.	BRANNY Daniel	C	G	Died 12.11.49
1817	Drummer	BRENNAN John	Medal only		Died 26.11.48
1641	Cpl.	BROWELL John	C	G	Wounded at Chilianwala
1177	Pte.	BROWN John	C	G	Died 19.10.49
2448	Pte.	CALLAGHAN Daniel	C	G	Died 10.9.50
2547	Pte.	CANNON John	C	G	Wounded at Chilianwala
340	Pte.	CARLIN Michael	C	G	Died 31.12.50
1676	Sjt.	CARR Henry	C	G	Died 11.7.50
649	Pte.	CARROLL John	C	G	Died 28.6.50
2045	Pte.	CARTY Michael	C	G	Wounded at Chilianwala
2492	Pte.	CAVANAGH John	C	G	Wounded at Chilianwala
	Asst.Surgeon.	CLARKE F.H.	C	G	Promoted Surgeon 83rd Foot 8.11.50
2226	Pte.	CLARKE Lawrence	C	G	Died 18.2.51
2218	Pte.	COLEMAN James	C	G	Wounded at Chilianwala
2441	Pte.	COLLINS Daniel	C	G	Wounded at Goojerat
2193	Pte.	CONNOLLY John	Medal only		Died of wounds at Sadoolopore 4.12.48
2435	Pte.	CONNORS Patrick	C	G	Died 23.10.49
936	Pte.	COOPER William	C	G	Wounded at Chilianwala, free discharge 16.2.50
2473	Pte.	CORNAIL William	C	-	Wounded at Chilianwala
2469	Pte.	CORNEIL Thomas	C	G	Wounded at Chilianwala
2349	Pte.	CORNWELL James	C	-	Wounded at Chilianwala
1946	Pte.	COULTER Patrick	C	G	Died 28.6.50
2728	Pte.	COUSINS James	Medal only		Dead
1704	Pte.	COWLES William	C	G	Wounded at Chilianwala, died 28.6.50
769	Pte.	COX Richard	C	G	Wounded at Chilianwala
956	Pte.	CRONIN Daniel	C	G	Died 17.11.50
2591	Pte.	DALEY John	C	G	Died 19.11.49
2537	Pte.	DALRYMPLE James	Medal only		
2015	Pte.	DALTON Michael	C	G	Died 7.7.50

1895	Pte.	DANCY Robert	C	G	Died 14.3.50
1108	Pte.	DANIELS William	C	G	To 98th Foot 1.9.49
2346	Pte.	DARLING Henry	Medal only		Died of wounds at Sadoolopore 6.12.48
1508	Pte.	DAVIS Isaac	C	G	Wounded at Chilianwala
2051	Pte.	DAVIS James	-	G	Died 19.3.50
1972	Pte.	DEVERAL Thomas	C	-	Wounded at Chilianwala
	Lieut.	DILKES W.C.	C	G	Died 4.6.49
2371	Pte.	DOUGLAS John	Medal only		Wounded at Sadoolapore, died 15.3.50
2718	Pte.	DOWEY Henry	-	G	Died 9.12.49
2409	Pte.	DRAPER Charles	C	G	Died 27.1.51
2240	Pte.	DUCK Henry	C	-	Wounded at Chilianwala
2237	Pte.	DUFFIELD John	C	G	Wounded at Chilianwala
2190	Pte.	DUGGAN William	C	G	Died 29.11.49
1029	Clr.Sjt.	DUGGAN Peter	Medal only		
2548	Pte.	DUNN John	C	G	Wounded at Chilianwala
991	Pte.	DUNN Michael	C	G .	Wounded at Chilianwala
625	Pte.	EAGAN Edmond	C	-	Died of wounds received at Chilianwala 14.1.49
1646	Pte.	EVETT William	Medal only		Died 3.12.45 Ramnuggur
2465	Pte.	FARRAHER Martin	Medal only		
632	Pte.	FARRAHER Michael	C	G	Wounded at Chilianwala
1837	Sjt.	FARRELL Michael	C	G	Wounded at Chilianwala, died 7.1.51
1561	Sjt.	FARRELL Otho	C	G	Wounded at Chilianwala
1391	Pte.	FEERICK Patrick	C	G	Wounded at Chilianwala
2285	Pte.	FENNER William	C	G	Wounded at Chilianwala
	Lieut.	FENWICK C.B.	Medal only		Retired - sale of commission 6.6.49
2468	Pte.	FLETCHER Edward	Medal only		Died 23.4.50
1937	Pte.	FLOOD Thomas	Medal only		
1253	Sjt.	FORD John	C	G	Discharge by purchase 19.4.50
2084	Pte.	FOSTER William	C	-	Killed at Chilianwala
2178	Pte.	FRAWLEY Jeremiah	C	G	Wounded at Chilianwala
2453	Pte.	FRAWLEY Patrick	C	G	Wounded at Chilianwala
1321	Drummer	FRASER Alexander	C	G	Died 17.10.49
2040	Sjt.	FRASER William	C	G	Wounded at Chilianwala
2246	Pte.	FYANS Charles	C	G	Died 2.1.51
1239	Pte.	GAVIN Martin	C	G	Died 3.9.49
1989	Pte.	GILES Charles	C	G	Died 11.2.50
2089	Pte.	GILMORE William	C	G	Died 27.4.51
2643	Pte.	GLENN William	C	G	Died 7.6.51
818	Pte.	GOODFELLOW Joseph	C	G	Wounded at Chilianwala
2066	Pte.	GORDON William	C	G	Wounded at Goojerat, died 16.4.49
2204	Pte.	GORMLEY James	C	G	Died 25.11.50
1662	Pte.	GRAY William	C	-	Killed at Chilianwala
1918	Pte.	GREEN John	C	G	Wounded at Chilianwala
1870	Pte.	HAGGERTY James	C	G	Wounded at Chilianwala
1800	Pte.	HALL William	C	-	Wounded
966	Pte.	HAMMONDS William	C	G	To 22nd Foot 1.4.51
2463	Pte.	HANLEY John	C	-	Wounded at Chilianwala

2167	Cpl.	HANLON George	C	-	Killed at Chilianwala
1585	Pte.	HARGRAVES Edward	C	G	Wounded at Chilianwala
2594	Pte.	HARNEW Samuel	C	G	Died 8.11.50
1497	Pte.	HARRIS Daniel	Medal only		Drowned at Buttalla 15.11.48
2012	Pte.	HARRISON William	C	G	Wounded at Chilianwala
2150	Pte.	HART Thomas	C	G	Died of wounds received at Goojerat 22.2.49
2270	Pte.	HART Michael	Medal only		
2438	Pte.	HARTNETT Timothy	C	-	Wounded at Chilianwala
2426	Pte.	HARTY Thomas	C	G	To 10th Foot 1.11.50
2310	Cpl.	HATFIELD Thomas	-	G	Died 5.8.50
1938	Pte.	HAYLIFFE John	C	G	Wounded at Chilianwala
2553	Pte.	HENDLE Edward	C	G	Wounded at Chilianwala
1921	Pte.	HENDRY John	Medal only		
2096	Pte.	HENDY Joseph	C	G	Died 27.11.50
2030	Pte.	HERLIHY John	C	G	Died 18.3.50
2077	Pte/	HESTER James	C	G ·	Wounded at Chilianwala
2413	Pte.	HOPGOOD Thomas	Medal only		Died 23.1.49
1810	Pte.	HORNBY William	-	G	Died 26.3.50
1939	Pte.	HUGHES David	C	G	Wounded at Chilianwala, died 5.11.50
2700	Pte.	HUGHES John	C	G	Died 4.5.50
2619	Pte.	HUMES James	C	-	Killed at Chilianwala
2290	Pte.	HUNT Isaac	C	G	Wounded at Chilianwala
836	Pte.	HUNTER Peter L.	C	G	Died 24.5.51
2554	Pte.	HURST George	C	G	Wounded at Chilianwala
683	Pte.	HYNES Thomas	C	G	Died 2.4.49
2498	Pte.	INGHAM George	C	G	Wounded at Chilianwala
1697	Pte.	JACKSON William	C	G	Died 13.10.49
2418	Pte.	JACKSON William	Medal only		Killed in action 3.12.48
2620	Pte.	JEFFERSON John	C	G	Died 4.8.49
1525	Pte.	JENKINS William	Medal only		
2555	Pte.	JENNINGS Edmond	C	G	Wounded at Chilianwala
Asst. Surgeon		JEPHSON William H.	C	G	To 9th Lcrs. 15.11.50
2556	Pte.	JOHNSON Henry	C	-	Killed at Chilianwala
2721	Pte.	JOHNSON John	-	G	Died 26.10.49
2260	Pte.	JOHNSON John	Medal only		
1934	Pte.	JOHNSON Matthew	C	G	Wounded at Chilianwala
949	Pte.	JOHNSON James	C	G	Free discharge 1.2.51
2018	Pte.	JONES William	C	-	Killed at Chilianwala
2558	Pte.	KENNEDY Christopher	C	G	Died 7.8.49
1077	Sjt.	KENNEDY James	C	G	To Depot. England 1/2/51
2022	Pte.	KENNEDY William	C	G	Wounded at Chilianwala
2168	Pte.	KENNY Michael	C	G	Wounded at Chilianwala
2491	Pte.	KENTLOW Henry	Medal only		Died of wounds received 18.1.49
2695	Pte.	KING James	Medal only		
2504	Pte.	KITCHEN George	Medal only		Killed in action 3.12.48
2598	Pte.	LANGSTON Frederick	Medal only		Died 15.6.49

2585	Pte.	LARKIN Patrick	Medal only		Died 9.9.49
2699	Pte.	LAVERY Patrick	C	G	Died 22.9.49
637	Pte.	LAVERY Peter	C	G	Died 31.7.50
2392	Pte.	LEARY Charles	C	--	Wounded at Chilianwala
1963	Cpl.	LESTER Robert	C	G	Wounded at Chilianwala
2314	Pte.	LESTER William	-	G	Died 16.6.49
	Lieut.	LEWIN J.St.George	C	G	Died 25.4.49
2505	Pte.	LINDSAY George	C	G	Died 12.8.49
1530	Sjt.	LONG Mark A.	C	G	Died 13.7.50
2612	Pte.	LOUGHRAY William	C	-	Severely wounded
2617	Pte.	LOUGUE William	C	G	Wounded at Chilianwala
Asst. Surgeon		LUCAS David	C	G	Died 28.10.50
2351	Pte.	LYNCH Alexander	C	G	To 98th Foot 1.4.50
1782	Pte.	MacINTOSH Alexander	Medal only		
1982	Cpl.	McALLISTER Henry	C	G	Died 16.11.50
2762	Pte.	McCORMISH Peter	Medal only		Missing after action at Fort Morarree 27.10.48
1476	Cpl.	McDONALD William	C	-	Died of wounds received at Chilianwala 20.2.49
2677	Pte.	McDONNELL Michael	C	G	Wounded at Chilianwala
979	Pte.	McDONOUGH Anthony	C	G	Died 17.5.50
539	O.Mst.Sjt.	McDONOUGH Stephen	C	G	Wounded at Chilianwala
1275	Pte.	McFADYEN John	C	G	Died 19.10.50
1194	Pte.	McGRATH John	C	G	Discharge by purchase 9.4.50
847	Pte.	McGRATT Patrick	C	G	Discharge by purchase 9.4.50
1212	Pte.	McHALE Patrick	C	G	Died 20.3.50
1976	Pte.	McKIBBON Shaw	C	G	Died 31.8.50
	Lt.Col.	McLEOD Alexander	C	G	Died 18.8.49
1178	Sjt.	McLEOD John	C	G	Died 15.7.49
1213	Clr.Sjt.	McLOUGHLIN Samuel	C	-	Wounded at Chilianwala, died 13.3.51
2743	Pte.	McMAHON John	-	G	Free discharge 16.2.50
492	Pte.	McMAHON John	Medal only		To Depot England 1.2.51
2702	Pte.	McMEEKIN Robert	C	G	Wounded at Chilianwala
1593	Pte.	McMURRAY Patrick	C	G	Died 9.6.49
2493	Pte.	McPHILLIPS Owen	Medal only		To England 16.2.50
2681	Pte.	McTAGGARTH Petrt	C	G	Wounded at Chilianwala
1987	Pte.	MADDEN Timothy	C	-	Died 10.2.50
2461	Pte.	MAHONY John	-	G	Died 11.10.50
2730	Pte.	MALLONY John	-	G	Died 31.3.51
2370	Pte.	MANNIX Michael	C	G	Died 8.12.49
1071	Pte.	MARA Lawrence	C	G	Wounded at Chilianwala
1682	Pte.	MARTIN Daniel	C	-	To 9th Lcrs. 1.9.49
1786	Pte.	MARTIN Robert	-	G	Dead
2284	Pte.	MARTIN William	Medal only		To Depot, England 10.5.49
1254	Pte.	MASON James	C	-	Killed at Chilianwala
	Capt.	MASSEY James	C	-	Severely wounded at Chilianwala
1473	Pte.	MATTHEWS Horatio	C	G	Died 9.2.51
2599	Pte.	MAXWELL James	Medal only		Died 9.5.49

61st Foot continued

2722	Pte.	MAYNARD Daniel	-	G	To 14th Lt.Dgns. 1.3.50
1953	Pte.	MEAKINS James	C	G	Wounded at Chilianwala, died 10.11.50
1196	Pte.	MELIA Anthony	C	G	Wounded at Sadoolopore
2566	Pte.	MOLOY John	Medal only		Died 13.11.48 at Guggur River
894	Cpl.	MOODY George	C	G	Wounded at Chilianwala
2184	Cpl.	MOODY Thomas	Medal only		Severely wounded, invalided to England 10.5.49
2057	Pte.	MOORE James	C	G	Wounded at Chilianwala, died 10.7.50
2159	Pte.	MOORE John	C	G	Wounded at Chilianwala
1451	Cpl.	MOORE Robert	C	G	Wounded at Chilianwala
2400	Pte.	MORDAUNT Augustus	C	G	Died 21.3.51
1154	Pte.	MULCAHY Dennis	C	G	Wounded at Chilianwala
1484	Pte.	MULCARE Michael	C	G	Wounded at Chilianwala
1648	Pte.	MULLINER Charles	C	G	Died 23.4.51
2406	Pte.	MURNANE James	C	G	Died 17.12.50
744	Pte.	MURPHY Thomas	C	G	Wounded at Chilianwala
1230	Pte.	NASH George	C	G ·	Wounded at Chilianwala and Goojerat
	Ensign.	NAZEL John	C	-	Severely wounded at Chilianwala, to 24th Foot 14.1.49
1364	Pte.	NELMES Thomas	-	G	Died 1.6.49
2017	Pte.	NEWSOME George	C	G	Died 6.5.51
1640	Pte.	NICHOLS John	C	G	Wounded at Chilianwala
958	Pte.	O'BRIEN James	C	G	Wounded at Chilianwala
2065	Pte.	O'DONNELL Thomas	C	G	Died 24.4.50
2108	Sjt.	O'GRADY John	C	G	Died 14.2.50
2273	Pte.	OLDIS David	C	G	Wounded at Chilianwala
2048	Pte.	ORR William	Medal only		
804	Pte.	PARKER Henry	C	G	Wounded at Chilianwala
2313	Pte.	PARKER Joseph	C	G	Died 15.9.49
	Ensign.	PARKES J.H.H.	C	G	Wounded at Chilianwala, died 29.7.49
1925	Pte.	PARSONS William	Medal only		Died at Ram-nuggur 1.12.48
2055	Pte.	PATULLA John	C	G	Wounded at Chilianwala
1980	Pte.	PAUL James	Medal only		
992	Pte.	PEACOCK Thomas	C	G	Wounded at Chilianwala
1878	Pte.	PEFFERS John Thos.	Medal only		Died 23.11.50
899	Pte.	PHILPOTT George	C	G	Died 7.9.50
2221	Pte.	PHILLIPS Thomas	C	G	Dead
634	Pte.	POLLOCK James	C	G	Died 21.9.49
1849	Pte.	POOLE James	C	G	Wounded at Chilianwala
2381	Pte.	PRATT Richard	C	G	Wounded at Chilianwala
1208	Pte.	PRENDERGARST John	C	G	Wounded at Chilianwala
2301	Pte.	PURCELL Henry	C	G	Died 27.3.51
2636	Pte.	RATCLIFFE John	C	G	Died 26.11.49
2673	Pte.	REGAN Peter	-	G	Transfered to 98th Foot 1.1.51
1862	Q.Mst.Sjt.	RICHES Richard	C	G	Died 8.6.49
2363	Pte.	RICHARDS William	C	G	Died 15.9.49
679	Pte.	RIELLY Patrick	C	G	Wounded at Chilianwala
2500	Pte.	RIELY James	C	G	Died 4.8.49
1656	Sjt.	ROACH Charles	C	-	Severely wounded at Chilianwala 25.1.49

2731	Pte.	ROBERTS Samuel	-	G	Died 11.6.50
2607	Pte.	RODGERS Samuel	C	G	Wounded at Chilianwala
2570	Pte.	ROLL Charles	C	G	Wounded at Chilianwala
1258	Pte.	ROLLINS John	C	G	Died 21.4.50
1725	Pte.	ROSS Alexander	C	G	Wounded at Chilianwala
2113	Pte.	ROUGHAN John	C	G	To 10th Foot 1.8.49
1855	Drummer	ROURKE Francis	C	G	Died 2.5.49
2420	Pte.	ROUSE James	C	G	Wounded at Chilianwala
2323	Pte.	RUGG Joseph	C	G	Died 13.1.50
1969	Pte.	RUMFORD Charles	C	G	Wounded at Chilianwala and Sadoolopore
2338	Pte.	RYAN John	-	G	Died 2.8.50
2571	Pte.	SANFORD Thomas	C	G	Died 27.8.49
2614	Pte.	SAUNDERS John	Medal only		
1984	Pte.	SCAIFE John	C	-	Wounded at Chilianwala
2019	Pte.	SCHOLDFIELD Richard	C	G	Discharge by purchase 11.10.50
2604	Pte.	SHACKLETON Samuel	C	G ·	Died 28.3.50
2697	Pte.	SHAW Isaac	-	G	Died 2.6.50
1304	Pte.	SHEA Daniel	C	-	Wounded at Chilianwala, died 28.11.49
2434	Pte.	SHEEDY Timothy	-	G	Died 13.8.49
1090	Drummer.	SHEPPARD Henry	C	G	Died 28.8.50
1114	Pte.	SHERWOOD Raplh	C	-	Killed at Chilianwala
2440	Pte.	SHINE Patrick	Medal only		Died 26.5.49
1171	Pte.	SMITH Henry	C	G	Died 23.12.50
1458	Pte.	SMITH James (2)	C	G	Died 7.6.50
2575	Pte.	SMITH William (3)	C	G	Wounded at Chilianwala
2230	Sjt.	SOUTHWOOD William	C	G	Wounded at Chilianwala, died 9.12.49
1499	Pte.	SPENCE James	C	G	Died 6.9.50
2415	Pte.	SPENCER James	-	G	Died 21.3.49
2357	Pte.	SPENCER John	C	G	Wounded at Chilianwala
2170	Pte.	SPRING John	C	G	Died 15.3.50
	Major	STEPHENS Frank John	-	G	Died 27.7.49
1257	Pte.	STEPHENS James	C	G	Died 10.3.50
	Ensign.	STRODE J.C.	-	G	To 14th Foot 7.6.50
1567	Pte.	TAYLOR James	-	G	Died 23.10.50
2577	Pte.	THOMPSON John	Medal only		
2075	Pte.	THORNTON Charles	C	G	Wounded at Chilianwala
2006	Pte.	TILL James	C	-	Died of wounds 26.2.49
2317	Pte.	TOBIN Henry	C	G	Died 19.12.50
2685	Pte.	TOOLAN James	-	G	Died 27.4.49
2384	Pte.	TOOMEY Michael	-	G	Died 22.11.49
1184	Pte.	TOUGHY Thomas	C	G	Died 4.11.50
2231	Pte.	TUCKLEY David	C	-	Killed at Chilianwala
1436	Pte.	TUCKWELL Thomas	C	-	Killed at Chilianwala
2459	Pte.	TURNER Edward	C	G	Wounded at Chilianwala
1377	Pte.	TURNER Thomas	-	G	Wounded at Goojerat
1228	Pte.	UZZLE Jesse	C	G	Wounded at Chilianwala
1975	Cpl.	WALSH Thomas	C	G	Dead

61st Foot continued

2277	Cpl.	WARD William	C	G	Died 5.2.51
1461	Pte.	WARNER James	Medal	only	Died 9.3.49
2059	Pte.	WATKINS Henry	C	G	Died 7.6.51
2174	Pte.	WELDON James	C	G	Died 17.10.49
2304	Pte.	WHITE John	C	-	Killed at Chilianwala
1853	Pte.	WILKINS John	C	G	Died 15.8.49
2121	Pte.	WILKINSON Richard	C	G	Died 1.11.50
1771	Pte.	WILSON John	C	G	Died 26.7.49
1307	Pte.	WOODING Richard	C	G	Wounded at Goojerat
	Lieut.	WOOLHOUSE John F.	C	G	Died 24.6.50
2215	Pte.	WRIGHT John	-	G	Free discharge 16.2.50

* * *

98th FOOT

2337	Pte.	ALLEN John	-	-	Invalided 21.8.49, to England 16.2.50
2394	Pte.	ALLEN James	-	-	Invalided 21.8.49, to England 16.2.50
808	Pte.	APPLEBY Noah	-	-	Died 30.10.49
868	Pte.	ARCHER James	-	-	Died 29.10.49
2056	Pte.	AULD David	-	-	Invalided 21.8.49, to England 16.2.50
1901	Pte.	BAKER John (1st)	-	-	Died 10.11.49
2555	Pte.	BANKS Henry	-	-	Died 4.12.50
2653	Pte.	BARLOW William	-	-	Died 25.11.50
2573	Pte.	BARRY John	-	-	Died 16.4.50
767	Sjt.	BICKNELL William	-	-	Invalided 21.8.49, to England 16.2.50
2000	Pte.	BLACKMORE James	-	-	Invalided 2.9.50, to England 1.2.51
1903	Sjt.	BOWEN David	-	-	Died 9.10.49
2389	Pte.	BUCKILING Joseph	-	-	Died 24.6.49
2995	Pte.	BURNS Joseph	-	-	Died 17.11.49
2420	Pte.	BUTLER James	-	-	Died 21.12.49
2253	Pte.	CAHILL Michael	-	-	Died 14.10.50
2910	Pte.	CAMP George	-	-	Died 9.5.50
2721	Pte.	CASEY Patrick	-	-	Invalided 2.9.50, to England 1.2.51
2203	Sjt.	CASSIN James	-	-	Died 14.2.51
2804	Pte.	CHAMBERS Joseph	-	-	Invalided 2.9.50, to England 1.2.51
2719	Cpl.	CLEEVE Charles	-	-	Died 14.7.50
2238	Pte.	CLEMENTS Edward	-	-	Invalided 21.8.49, to England
2839	NCO Staff	CONNERY William	-	-	Died 6.1.50
2521	Sjt.	CONNORS Michael	-	-	Died 1.12.50
2637	Pte.	CORCORAN John	-	-	Invalided 2.9.50, to England 1.2.51
1425	Pte.	COOKE George	-	-	Died 23.8.49
2845	Pte.	CRAWFORD Robert	-	-	Died 27.5.49
2625	Pte.	CROSS George	-	-	Died 2.6.49
1380	Pte.	CUPPER John	-	-	Died 2.6.49
1622	Pte.	DAVIS William	-	-	Died 21.9.49
2025	Pte.	DEACON Eli	-	-	Died 25.10.49

2454	Pte.	DENNIS George	-	-	Died 17.5.49
1558	Pte.	DEVITT Thomas	-	-	Died 20.10.50
2648	Pte.	DEWBERRY Thomas	-	-	Died 17.11.49
2870	Pte.	DONEHAM James	-	-	Died 15.9.50
2707	Pte.	DONOVAN Jeremiah	-	-	Died 14.10.49
2156	Pte.	DYER James	-	-	Died 26.12.50
2678	Pte.	EAGAN Charles	-	-	Died 5.8.49
2679	Pte.	ELLIOTT William	-	-	Died 6.10.50
867 NCO Staff Armr. Sjt.		FARRELL Michael	-	-	Died 25.12.49
2951	Pte.	FINLAY James	-	-	Died 8.9.50
847	Pte.	FITZPATRICK William	-	-	Died 25.10.50
2890	Pte.	FITZSIMONS Patrick	0	0	Died 23.1.50
2856	Pte.	FLEMMING Thomas	-	-	Died 26.10.49
2891	Pte.	FLYNN Cornelius	-	-	Died 31.10.49
2209	Pte.	FOSTER William	-	- .	Died 1.6.49
2748	Pte.	GARDINER Frederick	-	-	Died 27.2.51
2626	Pte.	GAVIN Bartholomew	-	-	Died 1.6.51
2291	Pte.	GETTINGS William	-	-	Died 11.12.49
828	Pte.	GOLDSMITH Ezekiel	-	-	Invalided 21.8.49, to England 16.2.50
	Capt.	GRANTHAM Francis	-	-	Died at Reshawar 15.3.51
2567	Pte.	GURNEY Richard	-	-	Died 10.2.51
2681 NCO Staff Sjt.		GUTHRIE John	-	-	Discharge by purchase
2543	Pte.	GUYATTE Henry	-	-	Died 12.7.50
2830	Pte.	HAGGIE Matthew	-	-	Died 16.12.49
2833	Pte.	HAILEY Peter	-	-	Died 19.11.50
865 NCO Staff Dr.Maj.		HANKINS William	-	-	Died 10.6.49
2623	Pte.	HANLEY John	-	-	Died 27.11.50
2392	Pte.	HART Philip	-	-	Died 5.6.50
1033	Pte.	HEBBARD Henry	-	-	Died 7.9.49
2659	Pte.	HEHEIR Michael	-	-	Died 7.6.49
2889	Pte.	HENNESSY Patrick	-	-	Died 28.9.50
1462	Cpl.	HENSON Thomas	-	-	Died 20.6.50
1545	.Pte.	HOEY Patrick	-	-	Died 17.3.51
2732	Pte.	HOWE Joseph	-	-	Died 23.5.50
663	Pte.	HURFORD James	-	-	Invalided 2.9.50, to England 1.2.51
2864	Pte.	JEFFERIES John	-	-	Died 7.12.50
1287	Pte.	JENKINS James	-	-	Died 26.10.50
2582	Pte.	KEAN John	-	-	Died 7.7.50
2384	Pte.	KELLY John	-	-	Died 10.7.49
2897	Pte.	KILCREIST Richard	-	-	Died 24.11.49
2800	Pte.	LAMBERT John	-	-	Died 13.5.49
2403	Pte.	LEDAIN George	-	-	Died 3.3.50
1625	Pte.	LEIVER Charles	-	-	Died 21.9.49
2290	Pte.	MACEY Henry	-	-	Died 25.1.51
1491	Pte.	MAHER Michael	-	-	Died 6.8.49

98th Foot continued

2706	Pte.	MAINS John	-	-	Invalided 30.8.49, to England 16.2.50
2527	Pte.	MALONE David	-	-	Invalided 21.8.49, to England 16.2.50
2739	Pte.	MARKS Joseph	-	-	Died 2.12.50
2805	Pte.	McASHNOG Hector	-	-	Invalided 21.8.49, to England 16.2.50
2925	Pte.	McCARTON Edward	-	-	Died 2.11.49
2725	Pte.	McDOWELL James	-	-	Invalided 30.8.49, to England 16.2.50
2122	Pte.	MERRITT Henry	-	-	Died 22.12.49
1334	Pte.	METCALF Thomas	-	-	Died 21.12.50
2916	Pte.	MITCHELL John	-	-	Died 18.11.49
2716	Pte.	MIZONS William	-	-	Died 21.11.50
	Ensign.	MOLLER Frederick	-	-	Died at Reshawur 20.9.50
2277	Pte.	MOODY John	-	-	Died 1.10.49
2085	Pte.	MORAN Michael	-	-	Died 13.8.49
2703	Pte.	MURRAY Patrick (1st)	-	-	Invalided 2.9.50, to England 1.2.51
1603	Pte.	NEAL Edward J.	-	-	Died 26.11.50
2865	Pte.	NOLAN Michael	-	-	Died 18.9.49
2606	Pte.	NOON Michael	-	-	Died 3.12.50
2877	Pte.	NURNEY Patrick	-	-	Died 29.12.50
1647	Pte.	OCKNEY John	-	-	Died 14.12.49
2818	Pte.	O'SHAUGHNESSY James	-	-	Died 4.10.50
1460	Cpl.	PALMER George	-	-	Invalided 2.9.50, to England 1.2.51
1409	Pte.	PARKER William (1st)	-	-	Died 20.9.50
2854	Pte.	PASSMORE Peter	-	-	Died 2.12.50
1900	Pte.	PEEDLE Joseph	-	-	Died 16.10.49
1402	Drummer	PHILLIPS John	-	-	Died 1.5.49
1985	Pte.	PITTMAN Thomas	-	-	Invalided 2.9.50, to England 1.2.51
2821	Pte.	PLUMMER William	-	-	Died 24.12.50
1593	Pte.	POWELL William	-	-	Died 19.12.50
2411	Pte.	POWER William	-	-	Died 5.10.49
2850	Pte.	RIELLY John W.	-	-	Died 25.11.50
2666	Pte.	ROBINSON James	-	-	Invalided 2.9.50, to England 1.2.51
1861	Pte.	ROWLEY Thomas	-	-	Died 3.12.50
743	Sjt.	RUSSELL Peter	-	-	Died 20.5.51
1882	Pte.	SANDLE George	-	-	Died 25.3.49
1690	Sjt.	SEABORNE William	-	-	Died 29.12.50
1816	Pte.	SEAGRAVES William	-	-	Died 14.8.49
2627	Pte.	SHREEVES George	-	-	Died 21.11.50
1863	Sjt.	SKELTON William	-	-	Died 14.8.49
2108	Cpl.	SMITH Andrew	-	-	Died 24.6.49
2234	Sjt.	SMITH Thomas	-	-	Died 14.2.49
1951	Pte.	SMITH Thomas	-	-	Died 6.4.49
850	Drummer.	SWEENEY Terence	-	-	Died 1.11.50
2892	Pte.	TAFFEY Morgan	-	-	Died 10.12.50
1077	Pte.	TEERS Henry	-	-	Died 15.10.50
2970	Pte.	TOWNSEND Joseph	-	-	Died 4.5.51
2089	Pte.	TRAVERS Michael	-	-	Died 20.12.50
1658	Pte.	TRUSCOTT George	-	-	Died 18.5.51

1854	Pte.	TUCKER John	-	-	Died 2.5.49
2058	Cpl.	VENABLES John	-	-	Died 21.10.49
1726	Pte.	VOWDEN Laurenace	-	-	Died 15.7.49
2837	Pte.	WALL Laurenace	-	-	Died 18.9.49
857	Pte.	WARD Stephen	-	-	Invalided 28.8.50, to England 26.2.51
973	Pte.	WELLINGTON John	-	-	Died 28.9.49
2385	Pte.	WHITE Robert (3rd)	-	-	Died 23.11.50
1962	Pte.	WILLIAMS William	-	-	Died 16.10.49
2040	Pte.	WRIGHT Joseph	-	-	Died 16.3.49

* * *

1 BOMBAY EUROPEAN REGT.

	Pte.	ANDREWS William	-	-	Died
	Pte.	ARMSTRONG Joseph	-	-	Died
	Pte.	BANISON Francis	M	-	Europe
	Pte.	BARRACLOUGH William	M	G	Died 13.1.51
	Pte.	BARNES George	M	G	Discharged by ourchase
	Pte.	BARRY David	M	G	Died 28.5.51
	Pte.	BERRY James	M	G	Discharged by purchase
	Pte.	BETHUNE John	M	G	Died 27.6.49
	Pte.	BINDING Isaac	M	-	Pensioner in Europe
	Pte.	BOARDMAN Henry	M	G	Died 26.3.51
	Pte.	BOSTON Edward	-	-	Dead
	Pte.	BOTTRIELL Richard	M	-	Europe
	Pte.	BRIDGE John	-	-	Dead
	Pte.	BRISNAHAN Michael	M	-	Died 28.5.51
	Pte.	BROWN Thomas	M	-	Dead
	Pte.	BUCK John	-	-	Dead
	Pte.	BURGESS John	M	-	Dead
	Pte.	BUTLER Geoffrey	-	-	Dead
	Asst.Surgeon	CALDER Alexander F.	M	G	Dead
	Pte.	CALLAGHAN Michael	M	G	Died 7.7.50
	Pte.	CAMPBELL Francis	M	G	Dead
	Pte.	CAMPBELL John	M	-	Europe
	Pte.	CAREY Alfred	-	-	Dead
	Pte.	CARROLL Richard	-	-	Dead
	Pte.	CATO Robert	M	G	Died 15.6.49
	Pte.	CHATFEALD William	M	-	Died 22.7.50
	Pte.	CLAYTON William	M	G	Died 3.3.49
	Pte.	COLLINS John	M	G	Died 17.6.49
	Drummer.	COLLINS Maurice	M	-	Dead
	Pte.	COMMON Richard	M	G	Dead
	Pte.	CONNOLLY Martin	-	-	Dead
	Pte.	CONNOR Timothy	M	-	Europe
	Pte.	CORBITT John	-	-	Dead

1 Bombay European Regt. continued

Pte.	COWAN John	M	G	Died 11.10.50
Sjt. Major	DAVIS Richard	M	-	Died 15.9.49
Cpl.	DELANEY Michael	M	-	Died 5.9.50
Pte.	DEVANNY John	M	-	Dead
Pte.	DOHERTY James	-	-	Dead
Pte.	DOUGLAS Henry	M	G	Dead
Pte.	DOYLE John	-	-	Dead
Pte.	DRISCOLL Jonn	-	-	Dead
Pte.	DRUMM James	-	-	Dead
Pte.	DUGGAN Daniel	-	-	Discharged
Pte.	DUGGAN Patrick	-	-	Discharged
Pte.	DUNLEAVY John	M	G	Died 8.5.49
Pte.	EASTON Joseph	M	-	Died 25.2.49
Pte.	ELLIS Robert	-	-	Discharged
Pte.	FITZMORRIS Patrick	M	-	Dead
Pte.	FORSYTHE Archibald	M	-	Died 5.8.49
Pte.	FRANKLIN John	M	-	Pensioner in Europe
Pte.	GIBSON Frederick	M	-	Europe
Pte.	GRAHAM William	M	G	Died 22.1.50
Pte.	GREARSON Robert	M	G	Dead
Pte.	GRIFFIN Patrick	M	G	Died 23.3.51
Pte.	GUINAR Patrick	-	-	Dead
Pte.	HAMIL John	-	-	Dead
Pte.	HANDS James	M	G	Died 4.7.50
Cpl.	HARROLD Henry	M	-	Died 30.11.49
Cpl.	HARROW Thomas	M	-	Died 10.12.49
Pte.	HAVERON Michael	-	-	Dead
Pte.	HAWORTH William	M	G	Died 16.8.49
Pte.	HAYES Denis	M	-	Europe
Cpl.	HINES John	M	G	Died 10.7.51
Pte.	HOLMES Thomas	M	-	Europe
Pte.	HORAN Thomas	-	-	Dead
Pte.	HORRIDGE William	M	G	Died 29.7.49
Pte.	HORRIGAN John	M	G	Died 13.8.49
Pte.	HORTON Samuel	-	-	Dead
Pte.	JAMES William	-	-	Discharged
Pte.	KEEFE Michael	M	G	Died 14.9.50
Pte.	KEITH William	M	-	Pensioner
Pte.	KELLY Donimick	M	G	Died 27.9.51
Pte.	KELLY James	M	-	Dead
Pte.	KELLY Patrick	-	-	Dead
Pte.	KENNEDY Thomas	M	G	Dead
Pte.	KETTLE William	M	G	Died 28.6.49
Pte.	LAWLOR Denis	M	-	Discharged in Europe
Pte.	LAWRIE Andrew	M	-	Dead
Cpl.	LEONARD William	M	G	Died 4.8.49
Pte.	LINTOLL William	M	G	Dead

Pte.	LOCKETT Henry	M	G	Pensioner
Pte.	LOW Michael	M	-	Dead
Pte.	LYONS Daniel	M	G	Died 3.8.49
Pte.	McCREA William	M	G	Died 15.3.51
Pte.	McDONALD Garrett	M	-	Dead
Pte.	McGUIRE Michael	M	-	Dead
Pte.	McKENNA Thomas	-	-	Dead
Pte.	McMAHON Patrick	M	G	Discharged, died 1.3.50
Pte.	McQUAID Terence	M	-	Discharged
Pte.	MALONEY John	M	-	Discharged
Pte.	MALONEY Michael	-	-	Dead
Pte.	MARA Cornelius	-	-	Dead
Pte.	MARTIN Isaiah	M	G	Died 22.3.50
Pte.	MARTIN Robert	M	-	Discharged
Pte.	MARSHALL William	M	G	Discharged by purchase
Pte.	MATES Robert	M	G.	Died 1.11.50
Pte.	MEEHAN James	M	G	Died 24.7.50, discharged
Cpl.	MEERS John	M	G	Died 24.5.51
Pte.	MIDDLETON Patrick	M	-	Died 20.11.49
Pte.	MILES James	M	-	Died 7.4.49
Pte.	MOFFITT John	M	G	Pensioner in Europe
Pte.	MONGIN Edward	-	-	Dead
Pte.	MOORE George	M	-	Discharged
Pte.	MOORE Richard	-	-	Dead
Pte.	MORRIS William	M	G	Died 8.12.49
Pte.	MORAN John	M	-	Discharged
Pte.	MOSSMAN Benjamin Alex.	M	G	Died 8.10.49
Pte.	MOYEAN James	-	-	Dead
Pte.	MULCAHY John	M	-	Discharged
Pte.	MULLINS John	-	-	Dead
Pte.	MURPHY Benjamin	M	G	Died 24.9.49
Pte.	MURPHY John	M	G	Died 23.8.50
Pte.	MURPHY Patrick	-	-	Dead
Pte.	MURRAY John	M	G	Discharged
Pte.	NELSON Robert	M	-	Deceased
Pte.	NESBITT George	M	G	Died 22.4.51
Pte.	NOWLAN Denis	M	G	Died 3.4.51
Pte.	O'CONNOR Patrick	M	-	Discharged
Pte.	O'DELL John	-	-	Dead
Pte.	O'DONNELL John	M	-	Discharged
Sjt.	OGLE George	M	G	Dead
Sjt.	OLDFEALD George	M	G	Dead
Pte.	O'LOUGHLIN Terence	M	G	Died 13.7.51
Sjt.	O'SHAUGHNESSY Michael	M	G	Dead
Pte.	PHILLIPS William	M	G	Died 23.2.50
Cpl.	POPE Samuel	M	-	Dead
Pte.	POTTS Charles	M	-	Dead

Pte.	POWER James	M	G	Died 18.11.50
Pte.	QUINLAN Lawrence	M	-	Dead
Pte.	RAMBURE Adolphus E.	M	-	Died 9.1.50
Pte.	REARDON Michael	M	-	Europe
Pte.	REDMOND John	M	-	Europe
Pte.	REYNOLDS John	M	G	Dead
Pte.	ROCK Jonathan	M	-	Died 15.12.50
Pte.	RUSSELL Thomas James	M	G	Died 13.10.49
Pte.	SCANLON James	-	-	Dead
Pte.	SEYMOUR Thomas	M	-	Dead
Pte.	SHAWYER George	M	-	Dead
Pte.	SHEA John	-	-	Dead
Pte.	SLATTERY John	-	-	Dead
Pte.	SMALL John	M	G	Died 20.10.49
Pte.	SMITH John	M	-	Europe
Pte.	SMITH William	M	-	Dead
Pte.	SMITH William	M	G	Died 5.11.49
Pte.	SPARK John	M	-	Dead
Pte.	STAPLETON Thomas	M	-	Died 10.7.50
Pte.	SULLIVAN John	M	-	Dead
Pte.	SWEENEY Patrick	M	-	Europe
Pte.	SWEENEY Timothy	M	-	Dead
Pte.	THOMAS Thomas	M	-	Dead
Pte.	THUMPKIN Patrick	M	-	Europe
Pte.	TILBURY Joseph	M	G	Died 18.6.50
Pte.	TIMMINS Martin	M	G	Died 21.9.51
Pte.	TREANOR James	M	G	Dead
Lieut.	WALKER H.T.	M	G	Dead
Pte.	WALSH James	M	-	Dead
Pte.	WARE James	M	-	Invalided to Europe
Pte.	WAETHERS John	M	G	Died 5.12.49
Pte.	WEBB James	M	-	Died 24.8.49
Pte.	WHITE James	M	G	Died 14.4.50
Pte.	WHITLAN Henry	-	-	Discharged
Pte.	WHITTY Patrick	-	-	Dead
Pte.	WILLIAMS Thomas	M	-	Europe
Pte.	WILLIAMSON James	M	G	Died 12.7.50
Pte.	WINTERBOTTOM John	M	-	Died 15.6.49
Pte.	WOOD John	M	-	Dead
Pte.	YEOMANS William	M	G	Died 13.6.50

* * *

2nd BENGAL EUROPEAN REGT.

Pte.	ANDOE Robert	C	G	Dead
Sjt.	BAILEY William	C	G	Pensioner
Pte.	BACKWELL William	C	G	Died 3.2.50
Pte.	BANKS George	C	-	Invalided to Europe

Pte.	BARKER James	-	-	Died 4.10.50
Pte.	BARRY John	C	G	Pensioner
Pte.	BLACKFORD William	C	G	Dead
Pte.	BOLAND Martin	C	G	Died 4.12.49
Pte.	BRENOCK John	C	-	Dead
Pte.	BRIGHTON Henry	C	G	Died 1.8.50
Pte.	BURK James	C	-	Dead
Pte.	BUTLER Lawrence	C	G	Pensioner
Staff Sjt.	CAIN Thomas	-	-	Dead
Pte.	CALLAGHAN Robert	-	-	Died 24.6.49
Pte.	CAPEL George	-	-	Dead
Pte.	CARROLL Joseph	-	-	Dead
Pte.	CARROLL John	C	G	Dead
Pte.	CHANDLER Thomas	C	G	Died 6.11.49
Pte.	CLARKE Joseph	C	G	Invalided to Europe
Pte.	CLEGG Alfred	-	-	Dead
Pte.	COLLINS Edward	C	G	Killed at Goojerat
Pte.	COLLINS Bartholomew	C	G	Killed at Goojerat
Pte.	COOPER John	C	G	Died 23.3.51
Pte.	CORR John	C	G	Dead
Pte.	CRATE Robert	C	-	Killed
Pte.	CROSS Thomas	C	G	Dead
Pte.	CROWLEY Patrick	-	-	Dead
Pte.	CUNNINGHAM John	-	-	Dead
Cpl.	DAMERY Thomas	C	G	Died 27.6.50
Pte.	DARNTON George	-	-	Dead
Pte.	DEE Patrick	-	-	Discharged by purchase
Drummer	DESMOND Hugh	C	G	Dead
Cpl.	DODD David	C	-	Dead
Pte.	DUFFY Thomas	C	G	Died 13.8.49
Pte.	DUNCAN Thomas	C	G	Died 15.7.49
Pte.	DUNNE Samuel	C	G	Died 18.8.49
Sjt.	EADE Luke	C	-	Died 17.11.49
Pte.	EARLEY Patrick	C	-	Died
Sjt.	EVERETT James	C	G	Died 16.7.49
Pte.	FENNELL Peter	C	G	Died 4.8.49
Pte.	FENTON William	C	G	Invalided to Europe
Pte.	FLANAGAN Thomas	-	-	Dead
Pte.	FLOOD William	C	G	Dead
Pte.	FOLEY Thomas	C	G	Invalided to Europe
Cpl.	FOUNTAIN Henry	C	G	Killed at Goojerat
Pte.	FOX William	-	-	Dead
Pte.	FOX Francis	C	G	Died 10.6.50
Pte.	GAFFNEY Patrick	C	G	Killed at Goojerat
Pte.	GRIFFIN Thady	C	G	Dead
Cpl.	HALORAN James	C	G	Invalided to Europe
Pte.	HANNON Thomas	-	-	Dead

Cpl.	HATTON William	C	G	Died 9.8.50
Pte.	HERBERT Thomas	C	-	Dead
Pte.	HIGGIN John	C	G	Invalided to Europe
Pte.	HOLDING Henry	C	-	Killed at Chilianwala
Pte.	HOLLAND James	C	G	Discharged by purchase
Sjt.	HOLLOWAY William	-	-	Dead
Pte.	HOLMES George	C	-	Killed at Chilianwala
Pte.	HOOKER George	C	G	Killed at Goojerat
Pte.	HORGAN Michael	-	-	Dead
Pte.	HOY John	C	G	Died 15.9.50
Pte.	HYNES Joseph	C	G	Died 2.9.49
Pte.	INGHAM Robert	-	-	Dead
Pte.	JACKETT Peter	C	G	Discharged by purchase 1.8.50
Sjt.	JENKINSON John	C	G	Died 24.12.49
Pte.	JOHNSON Thomas	C	G	Dead
Pte.	JONES George	-	-	Killed at Ramnuggur
Pte.	KEATING Jeremiah	C	-	Dead
Pte.	KEATING Michael	-	-	Dead
Pte.	KEAVENEY Michael	C	G	Discharged by purchase
Pte.	KEENAHAN Patrick	C	G	Died 15.9.49
Pte.	KELLY Stephen	C	G	Died 12.8.49
Pte.	KENNEDY Christopher	-	G	Died 4.9.49
Pte.	KEOGH Patrick	-	-	Dead
Pte.	KERR John	-	-	Dead
Pte.	KNAPP William	C	G	Dead
Pte.	LALLY Michael	C	G	Dead
Cpl.	LAWES Samuel	C	-	Killed at Chilianwala
Pte.	LITON Patrick	C	G	Died 8.6.49
Pte.	LOGAN John	C	-	Dead
Cpl.	LONE George	C	G	Died 11.9.49
Pte.	LOONEY William	C	G	Died 13.7.49
Cpl.	MACK Thomas	C	-	Dead
Pte.	MADIGAN Thomas	C	G	Invalided to Europe
Pte.	MAHONEY Cornelius	C	G	Invalided to Europe
Pte.	MANAHAN John	C	G	Dead
Pte.	MARCH Richard	C	G	Died 20.9.49
Sjt.	MAY Matthew	C	G	Discharge by purchase
Pte.	MITCHELL John	C	G	Died 3.11.49
Pte.	MOXSON John	C	-	Killed at Chilianwala
Pte.	MULDON Owen	C	-	Invalided to Europe
Pte.	MULLINS James	C	G	Invalided to Europe
Pte.	MULGUANY Francis	C	G	Invalided to Europe
Pte.	MULVEY Robert	C	G	Died 15.7.50
Pte.	MURPHY Edward (2)	C	-	Killed at Chilianwala
Pte.	MURPHY Jeremiah	C	G	Died 7.7.50
Pte.	McCORMICK John	C	G	Died 6.3.49
Pte.	McDONALD John	-	-	Dead

Pte.	McDONOUGH William	C	G	Died 28.5.50
Pte.	McGLOWAN Michael	C	G	Discharged by purchase
Pte.	McGRATH John	C	G	Invalided to Europe
Pte.	McKEY Patrick	C	G	Dead
Sjt.	McNAB Andrew	C	G	Died 30.10.49
Pte.	McNAMARA Thomas	C	G	Killed at Goojerat
Pte.	NAGLE John	C	G	Died 14.11.49
Pte.	NAGLE Martin	C	G	Dead
Pte.	NAGLE James	-	G	Died 17.8.49
Pte.	NEVILLE John	C	G	Died 20.11.49
Pte.	NEWTON James	C	G	Died 19.8.49
Pte.	NOWLAN Robert	C	G	Died 4.1.51
Pte.	OLPHERTS Thomas	C	G	Dead
Pte.	O'NEIL Joseph	C	G	Discharged by purchase
Sjt.	PATTISON Michael	C	G	Killed at Goojerat 21.2.49
Pte.	PEARSON John	C	-	Died 24.5.49
Pte.	PENDLEBURY John	C	G	Invalided to Europe
Pte.	PITMAN John	C	G	Died 17.12.50
Staff Sjt.	POUTAIN William	C	G	Died 15.12.49
Pte.	PROSSER John	C	-	Died 7.9.49
Pte.	QUINN Daniel	C	-	Died 2.8.49
Pte.	QUINLAN Thomas	C	G	Invalided to Europe
Ensign	RANNIE W.O.	C	G	To 32nd D.N.I.
Pte.	ROBERTSON Andrew	C	G	Invalided to Europe
Sjt.	ROBERTSON Samuel	C	G	Discharged by purchase 14.10.50
Pte.	ROCKCLIFFE Frans.	C	G	Discharged in England
Sjt.	ROSE George	C	G	Died 26.7.49
Pte.	RUDDEN Friday	-	G	Dead
Pte.	RYAN John	C	G	Discharged by purchase
Sjt.	RYAN John Thomas	C	G	Died 26.7.49
Pte.	SALMONI William	C	G	Invalided to Europe
Ensign.	SANDFORD D.A.	C	G	Dead
Pte.	SAUNDERS John	C	G	Died 26.4.50
Pte.	SCANLON William	-	-	Dead
Sjt.	SHANNON Jas	C	-	Dead
Pte.	SIMMONDS Samuel	C	G	Died 19.10.49
Pte.	SLOANE Christopher	C	G	Invalided to Europe
Lieut.	SPROT G.H.	C	G	Killed at Goojerat 21.2.49
Sjt.	SMITH John	C	G	Dead
Sjt.	SMITH Patrick	C	G	Dead
Cpl.	STIFF Richard	C	-	Invalided to Europe
Pte.	STRICH John	C	G	Dead
Pte.	SULLIVAN Thomas	-	-	Died 21.8.49
Pte.	TOBIN John	C	G	Killed at Goojerat
Pte.	TOPHAM Charles	C	G	Died 9.3.50
Capt.	VICARY Nathaniel	C	G	Retired

2nd Bengal European Regt. continued

Cpl.	WALDEN James	C	-	Killed at Chilianwala
Pte.	WALSH John	C	G	Died 8.12.48
Pte.	WALTON Richard Binks	C	G	Died 22.8.50
Pte.	WATKINS John	C	G	Died 4.9.49
Pte.	WATSON James Henry	C	G	Discharged by purchase
Pte.	WHITE John Henry	C	G	Discharged time expired
Pte.	WHOLEY Daniel	C	G	Dead
Cpl.	WILKINS George	C	G	Dead
Pte.	WILSON William	C	G	Died 29.7.50
Cpl.	WINTER William	C	G	Died 21.8.50
Pte.	WOGAN Christopher	C	G	Died 18.12.48
Pte.	WOODRUFFE Henry	C	G	Died 30.8.49
Pte.	WORRALL Edward	C	-	Invalided to Europe
Drummer	WRIGHT Samuel	C	G	Discharged by purchase

* * * . .

STAFF OFFICERS AT H.Q.

Brigadier General C.R. CURETON C.B., Commanded Cavalry Division. Half pay. Employed during the campaign in the Punjab to the date of occupation of Peshawur. Medal only. Killed in action at RAMNUGGUR on the 22nd November 1948.

Lightning Source UK Ltd.
Milton Keynes UK
UKHW052341011220
374464UK00002B/10